THE
FOOTBALL
COMPANION

A FOOTBALLING A to Z

Written by Michael Heatley

THE FOOTBALL
companion

This edition published 2004 by Igloo Books Ltd,
Henson way, Telford Way Industrial Estate,
Kettering, Northants, NN16 8PX.
info@igloo-books.com.

© Green Umbrella Publishing 2004
www.greenumbrella.co.uk

Printed and bound in China

ISBN 1-84561-030-X

Contents

Ajax

BELOW Ajax legend Johan Cruyff seen here in 1969

THE REPUTATION OF AMSTERDAM'S premier club, Ajax, is based as much on their reputation for nurturing young talent (first established under long-serving coach Jack Reynolds between 1915 and 1949) as the achievements of its senior team. Neeskens, Haan, Cruyff and Krol in the Seventies were followed by Rijkaard, Bergkamp and Van Basten who, in their turn were succeeded by Kluivert, Overmars and Seedorf.

The first quartet mentioned helped Ajax win the European Cup, predecessor of the Champions League, for three successive seasons from 1971, and also formed the backbone of Holland's World Cup Final team in '74. Counting domestic titles and the World Club Cup, Ajax held a 'nap hand' of five titles in 1972, a feat unlikely ever to be beaten. Their success was built on 'total football', a free-flowing style promoted by coach Rinus Michels allowing the players the tactical freedom to move away from rigid positional play.

Cruyff, who captained club and country, returned as coach in the mid

Eighties to win the European Cup Winners Cup in 1987, while a successful UEFA Cup campaign in 1992 made Ajax only the second club ever to have won the three major European competitions.

Louis Van Gaal guided Ajax to the European Champions League title in 1995, where they beat AC Milan 1-0, but the break-up of that winning team underlined the fact that Ajax have always been a selling club. The advent of the Bosman ruling has seen the likes of Reiziger, Davids and Frank and Ronald De Boer leave the Dutch capital for fame and fortune elsewhere.

Their move the following year from the De Meer Stadium into the sixth home in their history – the magnificent Amsterdam Arena, with its 55,000 seats – finally allowed Ajax to generate the revenue necessary to tie down their biggest names like current internationals Van der Vaart and Schneider to long-term contracts.

The club founded in 1900 by a group of Amsterdam businessmen who met for kickabouts on a Sunday had come a long way and, under coach Ronald Koeman, has plans to re-establish its name as a major European force. Former star striker Van Basten, who coaches Young Ajax, may hold the key.

AC Milan

THE SENIOR OF THE TWO MILAN clubs (Inter, with whom they share the San Siro Stadium, split from them in 1908), AC was founded in 1899 by a group of expatriate Englishmen seem-ingly as keen on playing cricket as football. By winning their first Italian league title two years later, the club nailed its sporting colours to the mast and further success followed.

Milan were in the vanguard of importing foreign players, Swedes Gunnar Gren, Gunnar Nordahl and Nils

Liedholm proving effective in the Fifties. The club's name was first engraved on a European trophy in 1963 after a star-studded team beat Benfica to claim the European Cup: managed by tactical genius Nereo Rocco, it included two future managerial legends in Giovanni Trappatoni and Cesare Maldini, with Gianni Rivera the midfield playmaker and Brazilian Jose Altafini the goalscorer. The Scudetto and Cup Winners Cup in 1968 were followed by a second European Cup win, 4-1 over Ajax, with Rivera voted European Player of the Year.

Having hit an all-time low in 1980 with demotion from Serie A due to financial irregularities, the club was restored to its former glory by media magnate and future Italian Prime Minister Silvio Berlusconi. His appointment of Arrigo Sacchi accompanied by investment in such superstar names as the Dutch international triumvirate of Van Basten, Gullit and Rijkaard led to great success in the late Eighties. Cesare Maldini's son Paolo was a defensive stalwart, and would lead the club into the new millennium as captain.

Sacchi's successor Fabio Capello continued the success, four Serie A titles in five years between 1992-96 setting the standard for others to follow. Victory over Barcelona in the 1994 European Champions League was particularly sweet, but they lost at the final hurdle the following year. 2003 saw them claim the ultimate European club title for the sixth time, with Shevchenko and Inzaghi the stars in an all-Italian clash with Juventus. It seemed fans of the Rossoneri still had much to cheer.

Arsenal

FOUNDED IN 1886, ARSENAL WERE known originally as Woolwich Reds, later as Woolwich Arsenal, and eventually simply as Arsenal. The Gunners have been in the top division of the league since 1919 although, as any Tottenham supporter will tell you, they should by rights have begun the first season after World War One in Division Two. They finished fifth in the old Division Two in 1915, but were mysteriously elected to Division One when League football recommenced after the cessation of hostilities. For many years afterwards, the team was labelled 'Lucky Arsenal'.

ABOVE Legends of the past and present. Herbert Chapman, hero of the Thirties, and Arsene Wenger, the current hero, shown in 1999 unveiling new signing Thierry Henry (not a bad buy!)

The Thirties was, until recently at least, the heyday of Arsenal Football Club. They were League Champions in 1931, 1933, 1934, 1935 and 1938 – a record run of five consecutive Championships being thwarted by Everton in 1932. Arsenal were runners-up that year. Their success was due in no small part to their legendary manager, Herbert Chapman, who had guided Huddersfield to similar success a decade earlier. The Gunners continued to be a major force after the Second World War, and have frequently featured in European competition since the late Sixties.

Ten years after Tottenham Hotspur did the League and FA Cup Double in

1961, their north London neighbours did it themselves – and went on to repeat the achievement in 1998 and 2002. They also won the FA Cup in 2003. The traditional rivalry between the sides still exists, but in recent times the Gunners have definitely had the upper hand. Keeper David Seaman did much to contribute to Arsenal's success during the Nineties, and more recently their squad of foreign nationals, plus one or two of the best home-grown players in the country, has taken the team to new heights. Manager Arsene Wenger, the Frenchman who never seems to see the occasional dodgy incident involving his own players, arrived at Highbury in September 1996. He inherited midfielder Dennis Bergkamp but he has brought in the likes of Freddie Ljungberg and Robert Pires, as well as prolific goalscorer Thierry Henry.

There seems little doubt that the current Arsenal team is set to become one of the best club sides in history. With a move to a brand new stadium at Ashburton Grove now well and truly on the cards, the future of Arsenal Football Club looks bright indeed.

The club went through 2003-04 unbeaten in the League, a feat last achieved by the 'Invincibles' of Preston North End back in 1888-89. However, theirs was a 22-game season, while the Gunners played 38.

BELOW Captain Patrick Vieira and Thierry Henry celebrate at White Hart Lane as Arsenal clinch the Premiership title

Beckham

DAVID ROBERT JOSEPH BECKHAM was born in Leytonstone, London, on 2 May 1975. All he ever wanted to do was to play football, and right from the beginning showed outstanding natural ability, combined with a willingness to train hard and learn. He was a Manchester United supporter and had no hesitation in signing for United when the time came, even though major local sides Arsenal and Tottenham were both keen to secure his signature.

'Becks' made his senior debut for United in 1992, but was briefly farmed out to Preston and had to wait another three years before he became a first-team regular. You might almost say he was a slow developer, but he certainly made up for it. Whether playing in central midfield or on the wing, the quality of his passing is almost unrivalled – and, when he gets them right, his free-

OPPOSITE David Beckham celebrates with Frank Lampard after England's 2-2 draw with Turkey saw them qualify for the 2004 European Championship

kicks have to be seen to be believed.

David Beckham made his England debut under manager Glenn Hoddle in September 1996, and it wasn't long before he became a cult hero. The hero-worship took something of a knock when he was sent off for kicking out at an opponent in a World Cup game against Argentina in 1998, but England fans have now forgiven him that little indiscretion – especially when his last-gasp free-kick won qualification to the 2004 European Championship.

Marriage to Spice Girl pop star Victoria Adams reinforced his celebrity status, something which helped sell thousands of red shirts with 'Beckham 7' on the back but perhaps did not go down too well with United manager Alex Ferguson. There was clearly some animosity between the two – a well-publicised dressing-room spat ending in a boot hitting Beckham above the eye – and, in summer 2003, Ferguson decided that Old Trafford could manage perfectly well without the player. He sold the current England captain to Real Madrid for £24.5 million. Whether or not Sir Alex made the right decision perhaps remains to be seen. A lot of United supporters think he was wrong.

ABOVE David and Victoria Beckham, football's glamour couple

Best

GEORGE BEST IS ONE OF FOOTBALL'S legendary figures, though the adjectives famous and infamous apply equally. Born in Belfast on 22 May 1946, the young winger came to Old Trafford as a 15-year-old. Manager Matt Busby put him into the Manchester United first team in September 1963 and he soon became, for a time at least, one of the greatest players the world had ever seen.

Best went on to score 178 goals in 466 United appearances. He was young, glamorous and fashionable and he had the world, as well as the ball, at his feet. A European Cup winner in 1968, his lightning speed and superb ball control meant that he was soon to be called up

BELOW George Best with Pat Crerand and Sir Matt Busby holding the European Cup, 1968

OPPOSITE One of George Best's many distractions outside of football – he owned his own boutique

for games eventually led to his quitting United in 1973. He was still only 27 but, even though he later made 42 League appearances for Fulham and also played in the United States, his career was effectively over. His international career was also over, after just 37 games for Northern Ireland.

Best, dubbed 'El Beatle' by the foreign press, was the first footballer to become part of the pop star/celebrity culture, and it did him no favours. When his playing days were finally over, he made a living through guest appearances and television punditry. He lives in Surrey, where his self-confessed problems with alcohol continue to cause him trouble despite a liver transplant.

by Northern Ireland and, for a few short years, there was no-one to touch him. In the end, however, it all became too much. Idolised by millions, Best pursued a lifestyle that attracted a great deal of adverse publicity and his game, as well as his health, began to go into decline.

George Best in the Sixties was probably more popular than David Beckham is today but, unlike Beckham, Best seemed doomed to self-destruction. Problems with women, problems with alcohol and problems with turning up

Brooking

HAVING FIRST TAKEN UP THE microphone in 1984, Trevor David Brooking, 56, has now been working for the BBC, on and off, for 20 years. He has become a very well known TV football presenter, although he is best remembered by those whose spiritual home is Upton Park, for his hundred-odd goals and 600-plus appearances for West Ham United.

A one-club man, midfielder Brooking spent his entire playing career with the Hammers, with whom he picked up two FA Cup winner's medals and headed the only goal in the 1980 Final against Arsenal. He made his England debut in 1974 and went on to win a total of 47 caps, being awarded an MBE in 1981. It's a wonderful record, and one of which he is justly proud.

Clever Trevor seems able to turn his hand to most things – he even wrote some book reviews for inclusion in the 1988 Liverpool-Wimbledon Cup Final programme.

More recently, as well as continuing his broadcasting career, he had two brief goes at temporary management with his beloved West Ham, where he was also a club director. The avuncular Brooking proved tougher than expected and

BELOW Trevor Brooking playing for West Ham in 1979

the supporters would have liked him to stay on, but he had other plans.

Trevor Brooking was involved with Sport England for eight years, and was Chairman for half of that time. The job had its ups and downs, and Brooking was at times very critical of the lack of government funding for sport in the UK.

Some believe that, with the England manager's post frequently being the subject of rumour and speculation, Trevor Brooking would be the ideal man to one day take up the poisoned chalice. For now, however, he is content with his latest job – that of the Football Association's Director of Football Development. Appointed early in 2004, he assists England's current Head Coach on all non-technical matters. He is not directly concerned with coaching, an area which does not seem to appeal very much to him, but of course he is very good at dealing with media people.

He also has responsibility for developing, promoting and improving the game at grass-roots level, and would appear to be just the man for this particular task. He will also be available to take over the top England job should a vacancy suddenly arise. Football has not heard the last of Trevor Brooking.

Charltons

NOBODY REALLY EXPECTED THE Charlton brothers, who were nephews of the legendary Newcastle centre-forward Jackie Milburn, to both play for England. Jack Charlton, born in Ashington, Northumberland in 1935, began and ended his career with Leeds United, making 628 League appearances and scoring 70 goals, but he did not make it into the England side until he was almost 30. Over the years he did, however, become a very efficient centre-half, but was playing mainly in the old Second Division and at first no-one took much notice. 'The Giraffe' as the lanky Jack was known, seemed doomed to remain in the shadow of his younger brother Bobby who, two and a half years his junior, was becoming a star forward with Manchester United.

Bobby was different. In all, he was to make more than 750 appearances for United, and score 198 goals in 606 League games. He came to prominence after the Munich air disaster, in which many of his Manchester United colleagues were killed, and he went on to play in a remarkable 106 internationals, scoring a record 49 goals. One of these games was the 4-2 victory over West Germany in the 1966 World Cup Final, by which time his brother had joined him in the side.

Jack played 35 times for England. When his playing career was over, he went into management, taking the reins first at Middlesbrough, then at Sheffield Wednesday and then, for just over a year, at Newcastle United. He was unhappy at Newcastle, but in 1986 took over the Republic of Ireland side and led his players to unprecedented success. In 1988, Ireland reached the European Championship finals, where they beat

England 1-0, and two years later Jack guided them to the last eight in the World Cup finals.

It often happens that fairly ordinary players make successful managers and that great players enjoy less success in the field of management. While no-one would suggest that Jack Charlton was an ordinary player, it is true that he was a far more successful manager than his brother. Bobby became manager of Preston North End in 1973, but his side was relegated to the Third Division in 1974 and Charlton resigned a little over a year later. He stayed in the game, run-ning a football school and becoming a director of Manchester United, but he will always be remembered for his fierce shot, his pace and his amazing body swerve – oh, and that trademark 'comb-over' hairstyle.

Chelski

CHELSEA FOOTBALL CLUB WAS founded in south-west London around 1905, when the owner of nearby Fulham FC decided not to relocate his team to the Stamford Bridge ground. The club was first promoted to the top division in 1907. Stamford Bridge was always a large ground and, in October 1935, a crowd of 82,905 witnessed a First Division match between Chelsea and Arsenal. Chelsea have spent much of their time in the old Division One or the Premiership, but have only once been League Champions. That was in 1955, but recent develop-ments suggest it may not be too long before the Championship trophy is held aloft once more.

For some years Chelsea's owner and chairman was Ken Bates, who believed that he could build a successful team, as

BELOW Chelsea owner Roman Abramovich (centre) and former Chairman Ken Bates (left) united in celebrating Chelsea's victory over Liverpool at Anfield, August 2003

well as a successful hotel complex, at Stamford Bridge. He constructed 'Chelsea Village' and the team began to do quite well too, but there were a few financial difficulties. And then came Roman Abramovich, a singularly young saviour. By coincidence, neighbours Fulham had, a few years earlier, been taken over by a wealthy chairman: Mohamed Fayed had put millions into Fulham and had taken the team into the Premiership, but this was as nothing when compared to the money Abramovich was to put into Chelsea.

Chelsea's new owner had become a billionaire following the fall of communism in Russia. He made his money from, among other things, oil and aluminium, and his personal fortune is estimated at close on £4 billion. He paid about £150 million for Chelsea in 2003, and spent more than £100 million on players within the first year. It's little wonder that the side is now known as 'Chelski' rather than 'The Pensioners'.

At one stage Chelsea fielded a team composed entirely of foreign players, but this has now changed. They may not quite have achieved perfection yet, but with England players like John Terry, Frank Lampard and Joe Cole in

their ranks, 'Chelski' look set to become one of the top teams of the early Twenty-First Century. They finished 2003-04 second in the Premiership and Champions League semi-finalists.

ABOVE John Terry (top) celebrates with Frank Lampard after Chelsea's 4-0 defeat of Lazio in Champions League 2003

Champions League

THE EUROPEAN CHAMPIONS LEAGUE came into being in season 1992-93 as a result of the two-leg knockout European Cup competition (founded in 1955) being reorganised into a hybrid League and knockout format. This had the benefit of guaranteeing those teams who qualified more than two games in the spotlight (and the accompanying financial rewards via television, etc), but the title of the competition was devalued in many eyes when clubs other than domestic champions were admitted.

The number of clubs that could be entered by any country and their entry point in the competition (there are three preliminary rounds) depended on the national association's position in UEFA's rankings. In a further dubious move, the third-placed teams knocked out in the group stages had the consolation of deferred entry into the UEFA Cup: Arsenal in 2000 and Celtic in 2003 both reached the Final of that competition after qualifying through the 'back door'.

But the Champions League goes from strength to strength, fuelled by media hype and television money. Marseille were the first winners in 1993, though victory was tainted by corruption allegations. Ajax's win two years later unwittingly showed the peculiarity of the system as they beat AC Milan twice in their group and a third time in the Final. Since then, Real Madrid have been the dominant force, notching three victories in the new format to go with six in the old European Cup (five

of these coming in its first five years).

British clubs, were free to participate in the new competition, having been re-admitted into Europe in 1991 after the Heysel tragedy, but it wasn't until 1999 that Manchester United engraved a UK name on the trophy – the third leg of a famous Treble including Premiership and FA Cup being achieved by two last-gasp goals from Sheringham and Solskjaer against Bayern Munich.

A second round of group matches was introduced to the competition, increasing revenue yet again, but was then scrapped. The 2003-04 season saw the three qualifying rounds followed by eight groups of four teams each, win-ners and runners-up advancing to the knockout stage.

Former French star Michel Platini, now vice-president of the French Football Federation, recently suggested a single competition replace the Champions League and UEFA Cup, with 256 clubs competing in a knockout format. Though this would increase each country's participation, it is unlikely to receive clubs' support for obvious reasons. The Champions League seems here to stay.

ABOVE Teddy Sheringham and Ole Gunnar Solskjaer celebrate their roles in Manchester United's historic 1999 treble

OPPOSITE Jean-Pierre Papin of Milan is challenged by Marcel Desailly and Jean-Christophe Thomas of Marseille during the 1993 Champions League Final

Double-winners

THE ABANDONMENT OF THE European Cup Winners' Cup may have robbed the FA Cup of some of its magic, but it will be remembered, especially at Preston North End, Aston Villa, Tottenham Hotspur, Arsenal, Liverpool and Manchester United, that the FA Cup remains one half of the most sought-after Double in the English game.

Preston North End were the first to achieve the feat, back in 1888-89, the first season of the Football League, at the end of the season when they won the League without losing a match and the Cup without conceding a goal; not for nothing were they known as the Old Invincibles. Aston Villa repeated their success in 1897, winning the title by 11 points and the Cup with a 3-2 win over Everton.

Since so many sides had come close during the next 60 years only to fall at the final hurdle, there were many who believed the feat to be beyond a modern side. In 1958 Danny Blanchflower, the Irish and Spurs captain, could talk of

BELOW All-conquering Arsenal salute their fans on the second of three Doubles to date

The fourth Double took another ten years to achieve, this time by North London rivals Arsenal. Whilst they have lacked the flair of the Spurs side of 1961, there is no doubting their resourcefulness, tenacity and workrate, factors that enabled them to overhaul Leeds United in the League (winning the League title by beating Spurs 1-0 at White Hart Lane in the final match of the season) and see off Liverpool in the Cup Final.

It was Liverpool who next lifted both major domestic trophies in one season, something of a personal triumph for player-manager Kenny Dalglish, who scored the crucial goal in the League match at Chelsea to secure the title. It will not be forgotten inside Goodison Park, for Liverpool's Double in 1986 denied their city rivals Everton their own Double. As well as finishing runners-up in the League they were on the losing side in the Cup Final, well beaten 3-1 on the day.

The arrival of the Premier League in 1992 may have changed the design of one of the trophies on offer but did not diminish the importance and relevance of the Double. Manchester United managed it twice in three years and might have made it three: Double winners in

LEFT Kenny Dalglish contributed to Liverpool's 1986 Double as both player and manager

little else, although over the next two years it appeared Wolverhampton Wanderers would be the next to achieve the feat, especially after winning the League title two years on the trot.

Spurs' exceptional start to the 1960-61 season (they won their first eleven matches and were unbeaten in 16) had them down as potential champions right from the off. By the time January came, Spurs were virtually out of sight in the League and could turn their attentions to the Cup. They were not at their best in the Final against Leicester, but the 2-0 win allowed them to complete the first Double of the modern era.

1994 and 1996, they were runners-up in both competitions in 1995.

It was Arsenal's turn again in 1998, knocking Manchester United down to second place in the League and easily overcoming Newcastle United in the FA Cup Final. The Double was won for the last time to date in 2002, again by Arsenal, as they continued to battle for domestic dominance with Manchester United. Whilst it may have taken 63 years before Spurs became the first side of the modern era to win the Double, six Doubles (or seven if we are to count Manchester United's 1999 Treble success) in the last 40 years has not diminished the achievement.

The League title and FA Cup double might be the ultimate domestic feat but it is by no means the only one. Nottingham Forest and Liverpool both lifted the League title and League Cup in the same season. Manchester City won the Cup Winners' Cup and League Cup in 1970, whilst Liverpool won the League and the UEFA Cup (twice, in 1973 and 1976) and League and European Cup in 1977 (and again in 1984, although they also won the League Cup to complete their own treble) before their 1986 achievement.

Derbies

ALMOST AS SOON AS THE NEW season's fixtures are published, fans across the country will quickly scan down their lists to see when they will be playing their nearest rivals. It is a custom that will be repeated in Bristol, Manchester, Liverpool, North London and Birmingham and everywhere in-between; the two fixtures against your local rivals will be the most eagerly awaited games of the season.

Close rivalry does not just exist within the town or city boundaries. Derby and Nottingham, Sunderland and Newcastle, Stoke and Port Vale and even down the League at Darlington and Hartlepool, the clashes between two close rivals are guaranteed to raise most interest. There is more than just three points or progress into the next round of the Cup at stake; invariably the winners will invoke bragging rights for the next couple of months, making the lives of their rival-supporting workmates, friends or even families hell until revenge can be gained.

In some cases, the rivalry between two clubs only exists off the pitch; there are countless stories of Spurs and Arsenal players living next door and giving each other a cheery wave as they make their respective ways to training! Similarly, Liverpool owe their existence to the fact that Everton, the original tenants of Anfield, upped sticks and moved across Stanley Park in protest at their rent being put up, the landlord forming Liverpool FC in their place!

In times of trouble, you can usually rely on your neighbour to help you out. Spurs shared Arsenal's ground during the First World War and the roles were reversed during the Second. Manchester United played at Maine Road whilst their ground was being rebuilt after bomb damage during the Second World War, and relationships between Everton and Liverpool were so cordial that the two clubs shared one programme for a time!

The rivalries may be intense, but there are always moments when they can be put in their place. That greatest of all managers, Bill Shankly, produced one of the greatest put-downs

of all time, and they even chuckle about it at Goodison – according to Shankly, when Everton lined up to meet dignitaries at the 1966 FA Cup Final, twelve months after Liverpool had lifted the Cup, the captain was asked where Everton was. "In Liverpool, Ma'am." "Of course," replied the Royal. "We had your first team here last year!"

BELOW Wayne Rooney and Jamie Carragher contest a 2004 Merseyside derby in typically committed fashion

Dribble

JIMMY GREAVES SCORED many goals during his career, more than anyone else during the modern era. A large percentage of these were scored inside the six-yard box, an area Greaves was particularly familiar with, pouncing on a loose ball here, a dropped ball there to net yet another goal. For many fans, however, the greatest he ever scored in the white shirt of Spurs was his mazy run half the length of the field against Manchester United in 1965 when he rounded two or three defenders and the goalkeeper before slotting calmly home.

Whilst all about him was pandemonium, Jimmy Greaves acknowledged the goal with his customary single hand raised salute (like a 1960s Alan Shearer). Whilst Greaves might not have felt the goal special at the time he scored it, countless replays should by now have convinced even him that he scored something magical.

Think of all the great goals that have

been scored during the near 125 years of the FA Cup. Whilst there will be one or two votes for Ronnie Radford's thunderbolt for Hereford against Newcastle United, or Norman Whiteside's curled winner for Manchester United in the final of 1985 against Everton, the two most oft-shown goals remain Ricky Villa's winner in the Final against Manchester City in 1981 and Ryan

RIGHT Ricky Villa with the ball at his feet – Manchester City beware!

OPPOSITE Inimitable wing wizard Stanley Matthews in full flight for Blackpool

Giggs' extra-time winner for Manchester United against Arsenal in 1999. Both involved a lot of dribbling, confusing the defence as the attacker turned first one way and then the other, never losing control of the ball or sight of the goal.

In Villa's case, the fact that the goal proved to be the winner lifted it to folklore status. In the case of Ryan Giggs' strike, keeping the Treble on track meant more to United's followers than either of the two winning goals in the Final against Newcastle United. Outside United followers, who could instantly recall either?

The undoubted master of the dribble was Stanley Matthews. The whole of his career was built around his exceptional ball control, never better displayed than in the 1953 FA Cup Final for Blackpool against Bolton. Blackpool scored three times in the final 20 minutes, Stan Mortensen completing a hat-trick, but it is Matthews' wizard dribbling to set up the win that has survived the passage of time.

England

ENGLAND'S STATUS AS THE country that gave the world football has given her a privileged position in the top ten of the world, even if her results on the field have been significantly lower down the table.

It is this reputation that causes opposition to raise their game whenever they face England. England's position as the birthplace of the modern game has meant every foreign side wanted to win at Wembley, more than any other venue in the world.

The long-redundant Home International Championships notwithstanding, a solitary World Cup win, achieved in 1966 at Wembley (and if England couldn't win it in their own backyard, where could they?) is not much to show for a hundred and forty years of endeavour. England's isolationist stance through the first fifty or so years of the 20th century and enforced absence during the 1980s, coupled with blind pursuit of tactics the rest of the world abandoned long ago, always seems to leave the English playing catch-up. Football's elite still seem to have a healthy lead, if the World Cup clash between England and Brazil in 2002 was anything to go by, even if there are the occasional moments when the gap seems to narrow, as evidenced by the 5-1 victory over Germany en route to the 2002 finals.

Part of the problem lies with achievement always falling well short of expectation. England were expected to retain the 1970 World Cup but fell apart in the quarter-final against West Germany although, had Gordon Banks been well enough to play, they should have advanced to the semi-final at least. Whether they would have beaten the Brazilians in the Final is a matter of some debate. They were then expected to at least qualify for the finals in 1974 and 1978, but allowed the Poles and Italians respectively to ease them out.

After stuttering through qualification to the 1982 finals, they started impressively and got steadily worse, running out of steam in the crucial match against Spain. Their performance in 1986, when they were ragged to begin with and got better, finally beaten by a dubious handball goal from Maradona in the quarter-final, followed the same pattern, flattering to deceive. Indeed, about the only tournament in which England did better than expected was 1990 in Italy, when they made the semi-finals but lost out on penalties to their nemesis Germany. After missing out in 1994, England have returned to the quarter-finals but no further in the last two tournaments.

It is much the same story in the European Championships, where England have reached the semi-finals on two occasions, in 1968 when they were beaten 1-0 by Yugoslavia (during which Alan Mullery became the first England player to be sent off) and 1996, when the tournament was played in their own backyard. Once again, they were beaten in the semi-final on penalties by the Germans.

It has always been said that the British in general and English in particular are gracious losers. There is a good reason for this – we've had more experience than most other nations! Who knows, perhaps that is all about to change. As Lord Nelson would say, 'England expects.'

BELOW England's finest hour, the World Cup win of 1966, is long overdue a repeat

European Championships

WHILST MOST RECORD BOOKS tend to show European competition began in 1955 with the launch of the European Champions' Club Cup, there were plenty of earlier competitions that are worthy of note.

The Austria/Habsburg Challenge Cup, launched in 1897 and open to any club within the Habsburg Monarchy (although in reality only clubs from Vienna, Prague and Budapest took part) is generally considered the earliest and ran until 1911.

Austria proved to be the organisational force behind the next major competition, the Mitropa Cup, which involved two teams each from Hungary, Austria, Czechoslovakia and Yugoslavia and launched in 1927. More countries were admitted in the years preceding the Second World War.

It was Henri Delaunay, secretary of the French Football Federation that first put forward the idea of the European Championships in 1956 (hence the actual trophy is named after him).

ABOVE Henri Delaunay, European visionary

Invitations to the member countries were extended for the inaugural competition to commence in 1958, but interest was somewhat lacking, with all four British countries and West Germany among the most noticeable absentees.

The semi-finals and Final were to be played in Paris in July 1960, with Yugoslavia ousting the hosts 5-4 and the Russians beating Czechoslovakia 3-0 to book their place in the showdown. Although Yugoslavia took the lead, the Russians finally won after extra time 2-1 to become the first winners of the Henri Delaunay Cup.

The competition has grown in both size and stature since those early days, flourishing in spite of one or two problems along the way – Greece refused to play Albania in 1964 since the two countries were technically at war! The format of group matches was introduced in 1968, along with a new name, the UEFA European Football Championship (the trophy itself was retained), although to begin with the group winners progressed into a two-legged quarter-final.

The semi-finals and Final were single-match affairs to be played in one country until 1980, when eight

countries competed in two groups and the winners played off for the final. By 1992 the top two in each group qualified for the semifinals, a year made notable by the fact that Denmark, a last-minute replacement for the war-torn Yugoslavia, defied all the odds to beat Germany in the Final.

The collapse of the communist countries in Eastern Europe swelled UEFA's membership ranks to 48 and a new format was devised for the 1996 competition. The top 16 qualifiers would now be placed into four groups of four (similar to the World Cup finals), with the top two teams progressing into the quarter-finals.

This format has been retained ever since as the European Football Championship has blossomed from its uncertain beginnings into the second most important event on the international football calendar.

Eriksson

THERE HAVE BEEN MANY controversial managerial appointments over the years, usually when a player who made his reputation with one club turns up to manage their rivals. But few appointments have created the furore that surrounded Sven Goran Eriksson's appointment as England head coach.

There are those who believe that the job, like that of the American President, should only go to someone born in the

ABOVE LEFT Captain Didier Deschamps proudly displays France's European Championship trophy, 2000

LEFT Impassive Sven the Swede keeps his thoughts to himself

country. But England had run out of candidates after the departures of Glenn Hoddle and Kevin Keegan, the others not yet up to the rigours of the job.

England was to be Sven's first national appointment too, but he had already cut his teeth in the Swedish, Portuguese and Italian game, winning domestic titles with IFK Gothenburg, Benfica and Lazio and the Italian Cup with both Roma and Sampdoria. Indeed, the Italian coaching fraternity nicknamed him The Iceman as a nod to his unflappable nature.

More recently there has been speculation that he could be off before his England contract expires to return to club management, with Chelsea making the loudest noises. On the plus side, his achievements with England, such as they are (no trophy wins at the time of writing, but only one defeat in a meaningful match) has pushed the national side up the merit table. On the negative side, his teams are often described as being bland, but is this Sven Goran Eriksson's fault – he can only work with the players at his disposal, and until Ronaldo, Thierry Henry et al discover English grandparents, Sven has to get the best out of what he has.

When Eriksson finally calls time on his England adventure, there will be much analysis of his career. Was he a successful manager? Was he a lucky manager? At present, the answer to both questions is yes. He has been more successful than we had a right to expect, qualifying for the 2002 World Cup as group winners when, at the time of his appointment, play-offs were all we could expect. He has made his own luck, piloting England to that 5-1 win in Germany. If that combination of good luck and management continues his nationality will never be an issue again.

RIGHT Sven on the training pitch with Dyer and Lampard

Ferguson

GRITTY GLASWEGIAN ALEX Ferguson failed to make headlines in a playing career that spanned six clubs north of the border and peaked at Rangers between 1967-69, but found unparallelled success as a manager.

Starting at St Mirren in 1975, he broke the mould of Scottish football while manager of Aberdeen, winning three Championships, four Scottish Cups and the European Cup Winners Cup in six years. Along with Dundee United, the Dons under Ferguson smashed the Old Firm (Celtic and Rangers)'s monopoly of honours. He joined Manchester United in 1986 as a somewhat dour successor to the flamboyant Ron Atkinson. His first three seasons brought little – chairman Martin Edwards resisting the call for Fergie's head after a 5-1 walloping by neighbours City in 1989 – but after the

ABOVE Depite his penchant for accurate timekeeping, Sir Alex isn't ready for his gold watch just yet

Red Devils took off again with an FA Cup win in 1990 they dominated the English domestic game in the way Liverpool dominated the late 1970s and 1980s.

Ferguson increasingly featured home-grown youngsters like David Beckham, Paul Scholes, Nicky Butt and the Neville brothers, Gary and Phil alongside the big-name buys, and these, along with David Beckham, would become England international regulars. United recorded two League and Cup Doubles, the first English club ever to achieve the feat, and took four of the first five Premierships, but critics claimed the retirement of Eric Cantona would bring an end to the glory days. Fergie and his Fledglings (the new Busby Babes) proved the doubters wrong as in 1999 they swept all before them en route to an historic Treble of Premiership, FA Cup and European Cup. A knighthood was the wily Scot's reward as his team carved an unique place in the record books with their clean sweep of domestic and European honours.

Ferguson's premature (and since rescinded) decision to retire at the end of 2001-02 led to morale problems that season as Arsenal overtook them, while his personality clash with David Beckham arguably weakened the team sufficiently to ensure they could not retain the Premiership title in season 2003-04.

But Ferguson, a working-class lad who made good, still puts in 18-hour days at the United training ground and, when he fell out with club shareholders John Magner and JP McManus over stud rights to the racehorse Rock Of Gibraltar, was backed by 100 per cent of United fans. Now into his sixties, like 'Rock' in his prime, he shows no sign of giving up.

RIGHT The legendary White Horse Cup Final of 1923 between Bolton and West Ham was remembered for its over-capacity crowd

FA Cup

THE FA CUP IS WIDELY REGARDED as being the world's finest domestic knockout competition. Some say it is less important than it once was – but try telling that to the fans, or indeed, to the players. It all began in 1872, when the competition was instituted for what were then amateur clubs. The first winners were The Wanderers, and they repeated their success in 1873. Next, Oxford University, and then the Royal Engineers held the trophy aloft, before The Wanderers did it again for three successive seasons.

As professionalism began to take a hold, The Wanderers wandered off into the sunset and in 1884 the first of the 'modern' clubs – Blackburn Rovers – won the Cup. They also won it three years running. In its early days, the Cup Final was played at a variety of locations, including The Oval but at last, in 1923, it found a permanent home at the Empire Stadium, Wembley.

The Cup Final remained synonymous with Wembley until 2001, when it moved on a temporary basis to the Millennium Stadium, Cardiff. It will return to Wembley when the new stadium is finally completed.

The FA Cup has always provided shock results but, in modern times, no team outside the top two divisions has won the trophy. However, Tottenham Hotspur did become the first non-League club to win it after the formation of the Football League, their success coming in 1901. Manchester United currently hold the record for the highest number of FA Cup wins, having lifted the trophy on 11 occasions after easily beating First Division Millwall 3-0 in 2004.

Ironically, United withdrew from the competition in 1999-2000 to pursue the World Club Championship in Rio de Janeiro, thus refusing to defend the trophy they had won the previous season as part of an historic Treble. Happily, the FA continue to value and protect the competition's prestige, and it is good to report that, unlike the League Cup, the trophy has never yet been allowed to take a sponsor's name directly.

BELOW The 2003 FA Cup Final was the third at the event's temporary Millennium Stadium, Cardiff, home

Floodlights

THE FOOTBALL LEAGUE DID NOT approve the use of floodlights until the mid 1950s, but the first English football match to be played under them took place at Bramall Lane, Sheffield in 1878. Dynamos were used to power the lights, which were attached to wooden towers.

Floodlights meant that games could be played at any time during the dark winter days. There were however many problems with reliability, and floodlighting failed to really take off until after the First World War. Even then, the Football Association was not keen on the idea, and it tried to prevent clubs from using them. After the Second World War, the pressure from clubs increased, and the FA gave way.

The first League club to install lights was Third Division (South) Swindon Town. They switched on their illuminations for a friendly in 1951, and many of the bigger clubs soon copied them. A few FA Cup games were subsequently played under lights, but the first Football League game to be floodlit took place in 1956, when Portsmouth entertained Newcastle.

Within a few years only a couple of First Division grounds were without floodlights. The lights were mainly mounted on towers, one at each corner of the ground, and many of these towers survive to this day. Tower lighting does however tend to illuminate much of the surrounding area, often to the annoyance of local residents, and in more recent years there has been a move towards lighting along the edges of stand roofs. Floodlighting is today a very sophisticated science.

RIGHT Floodlights at Charlton's Valley ground pierce the South London gloom

Giggs

IF RYAN GIGGS WAS BORN IN THE wrong generation, he has more than made his mark on football in general and Manchester United in particular. A throwback of some 20 or 30 years, his dazzling runs on the wing for United have created chance after chance for a grateful forward line for the last thirteen or so years.

Born in Cardiff on 29th November 1973, Ryan joined United straight from school and made his debut during the 1990-91 season. The following season he made 38 appearances and scored four goals as United battled with Leeds United for the League title, finally having to settle for runners-up spot. Compensation of sorts was reached in the Rumbelows Cup, with United beating Nottingham Forest 1-0 in the Final to enable Ryan to collect his first

winners medal. Since then he has become the most decorated player in the domestic game. Although he represented England at youth level, Ryan

BELOW Ryan Giggs concludes his legendary FA Cup dribble of 1999 with an ice-cool finish.

later opted to turn out for Wales and has gone on to win over 40 full caps for the country of his birth. But, with Wales having failed to qualify for any of the major tournaments during his career, he has been unable to display his talents on the world stage. In many ways, this mirrors a previous United wingman, George Best, who also never played in a major international tournament.

Whilst Giggs is chiefly a goal supplier, he has also weighed in with more than a few goals of his own, netting the 100th of his United career in August 2002. Perhaps his most celebrated goal was the winner in the FA Cup semi-final replay against Arsenal in 1999 when he ran virtually the length of the field, netting past a bemused David Seaman.

There was a time early on during the 2003-04 season that United fans began to turn against Ryan Giggs, feeling that he was losing some of his pace and therefore his usefulness to the side, but perhaps he was feeling the loss of David Beckham. Having made over 500 appearances for the Reds, one suspects he still has a couple of hundred more in him before he is allowed to leave.

Good news for United, bad news for everyone else!

OPPOSITE Giantkiller turned coach Jim Montgomery prepares Scarborough's keeper Leigh Walker to face Chelsea, 2004

BOTTOM Hereford's Ronnie Radford cools his shooting boots, 1972

Giantkillers

IF THERE IS ONE THING THAT encapsulates the magic of the FA Cup, it is giantkilling. When the draw is made, pitting some non-League or Third Division club at home to a Premiership club, interest is heightened by the prospect of a giantkilling.

It has always been this way. Arsenal may have one of the best records in the FA Cup, but in Walsall they will always remember the day back in 1933 when the Third Division side beat the League Champions 2-0 in the FA Cup third round. In fact, the result was such a shock that Arsenal manager Herbert Chapman singled out Tommy Black as the villain of the day, selling him to Plymouth Argyle within a week!

Whilst form and ability will even out over the course of a League season, they often count for nothing in a one-off match. An unfamiliar pitch often plays its part, as Sunderland found to their cost in a Cup tie at Yeovil in 1949 – although Sunderland took the lead, Yeovil's players were better equipped to cope with the sloping pitch and ran out 2-1 winners on the day. On other occasions, the elite cannot even use this as an excuse – Arsenal were held to a 2-2 draw at Highbury by Bedford in 1956 and Newcastle were held to a similar scoreline at home to Hereford in 1972.

The replays both ended 2-1, but whilst Arsenal managed to overcome their non-League opposition, Newcastle were on the receiving end of one of the biggest cup upsets of all time, with Ronnie Radford netting a thunderbolt that has been shown on television prior to just about every round of the FA Cup ever since. As a result of their exploits, Hereford were subsequently voted into the League, as were Wimbledon as a result of victory over Burnley in 1975.

According to the form book, media and experts, the 1973 FA Cup Final could only end in a Leeds United victory over Second Division Sunderland, but on the day goalkeeper Jim Montgomery played the game of his long and illustrious career and Ian Porterfield netted the only goal to register the biggest Cup Final upset ever.

With the big clubs keen to reduce the number of matches they have to play, there's been talk of the FA Cup following its League counterpart and doing away with replays, all matches to be decided on the day. This would be sad, for what makes the FA Cup so magical is the regularity with which the underdog is able to upset his bigger rival.

Goals

IT IS NOT A SIGHT seen on too many parks and fields these days, largely because most parks and fields already have goalposts erected, but not so long ago kids desperate for a game of football would grab anything to mark out a goal – the phrase jumpers for goalposts will invoke an instant reaction in anyone over 30!

As is fairly well known, football in England began as an inter-village game involving hundreds of players per side. There were no goals as such; the ball just got kicked and carried between two villages, up and down streams and rivers with no real target in sight.

Although the Football Association came into being in 1863, it was not until three years later that the FA refined the ruling on goal posts, passing the resolution that 'the goals shall be upright posts, eight yards apart, with a tape across them, eight feet from the ground.' This ruling remained in place for a further eleven years when, after consultation with the Sheffield FA and in a desire to get a uniform set of rules in place, the wording was amended to read 'with a tape or bar across them, eight feet from the ground.'

In 1889 JA Brodie of Liverpool patented goal nets, with a match in Bolton between two local sides on New Year's Day 1890 being the first occasion they were used. The next year was spent trying out the new invention, with the FA keen observers. Finally, in February 1891, the FA minutes reported:

ABOVE RIGHT Geoff Hurst's controversial third goal in England's World Cup victory in 1966 did not hit the back of the net – but did it cross the line?

38 | THE LITTLE BOOK OF FOOTBALL

"Mr JA Brodie was interviewed on the subject of his goal-nets. The following resolution was carried: That the Council approve of the use of nets as under Mr Brodie's patent, but cannot take any steps to amend the rule so as to make their use compulsory to until some satisfactory arrangement can be made with the patents as to prices to be charged to clubs." Even now the use of nets is still optional.

In 1996 FIFA announced plans to make the goals wider by the diameter of two balls and taller by the diameter of one ball, agreeing to listen to opinion on the matter. Although the planned change would have taken place immediately after the 1998 World Cup, these plans were subsequently dropped.

No matter what size the goal is, or whether the nets are optional or compulsory, there is still a great feeling to be derived from scoring a goal, either in a town park or at Hampden Park. What a shame that those villagers of so many years ago never got to experience the thrill!

BELOW A corner flag but no goalposts in sight in this early game of football

Henry

THIERRY DANIEL HENRY WAS born in the Paris suburb of Chatillion on 17th August 1977. He was a schoolboy prodigy with Versailles, and was signed up by Monaco at the age of 13. He remained there until 1997, when Monaco won the French First Division title. Henry then moved to Italy and Juventus, before Arsene Wenger brought him to England by signing him for Arsenal in 1999 for a reported fee of £10.5 million.

Henry was originally a winger. He made his debut for Monaco a fortnight after his 17th birthday, and he played for France for the first time in 1997. He picked up a World Cup winner's medal in 1998, not long before his move to Juventus, but things then began to go wrong for him and it looked as though his early promise would not be fulfilled. He was not an automatic choice for the Juventus first team and, as a winger, he scored just 3 goals in 16 appearances. Wenger however, who had originally worked with Henry at Monaco, saw something that others failed to.

He converted him into a striker and, although it took some while, Thierry Henry went on to become one of the most prolific goalscorers in the Premiership. Having helped his country win Euro 2000, he then helped Arsenal achieve the club's third ever Double in 2002 and was the Premiership's top scorer.

Thierry Henry would appear to have just about everything. He can show a tremendous turn of speed and his reading of the game is immaculate. Add to this the fact that he is also a creator of goals, an opportunist striker and a great penalty taker, and you have a man who became the first to win consecutive PFA Player of the Year titles in April 2004.

Henry is supported in the Arsenal side by midfielders Robert Pires, Freddie Ljungberg, Patrick Viera and Edu, and by fellow strikers Dennis Bergkamp and, more recently, Jose Antonio Reyes, a 21 year-old from Sevilla who cost Arsenal upwards of £17.5 million. Between them, they make a formidable combination.

LEFT Henry and Chelsea's Melchiot battle for supremacy. Though Chelsea knocked Arsenal out of Europe, the Gunners took the 2003-04 Premiership

Hat-trick

A HAT-TRICK IN FOOTBALL IS when a player scores three goals in a game and claims the match ball. The term is borrowed from cricket, where a new hat would be given to a bowler who claimed three wickets with consecutive balls. (Others claim that, in the days when footballers got the bus to the match with fans, passing round of a hat to collect money was a way of rewarding a player for his on-field efforts.) Goals do not need to be scored consecutively, however, as with wickets in cricket.

Arguably the most famous hat-trick ever is the one Geoff Hurst scored for England at Wembley in the 1966 World Cup

BELOW Bournemouth's James Hayter celebrates his 'three in two' feat

Final to secure the trophy for the home nation. Though the first in a Final, it was not the first to be scored in the final stages: that was by Guillermo Stabile of Argentina in their 6-3 win over Mexico in 1930. The first by a substitute was claimed by Laszlo Kiss of Hungary in a match against El Salvador in 1982. Last but not least, Gabriel Batistuta of Argentina became the only player to date to have scored a hat-trick in successive World Cup tournaments against Greece in 1994 and Jamaica four years later.

Returning to England, Spurs' Willie Hall entered the record books by scoring three goals in four minutes against Northern Ireland in a Home International Championship match in November 1938. England were 1-0 up before Hall's 36, 38 and 40th-minute first-half goals. He scored twice more in the second half to notch up five of England's seven without reply.

More recently, Bournemouth striker James Hayter broke English records when he notched three goals in two minutes 20 seconds for Bournemouth against Wrexham in February 2004. This was all the more remarkable because he had come on as a second-half substitute and scored his first with his first touch of the ball. His parents who live on the Isle of Wight had left Dean Court to catch the ferry, believing he was unlikely to feature in the match, and missed the action.

The Premiership record is held by Robbie Fowler, who notched a four minute 35 second treble for Liverpool against Arsenal in 1994. For the record, James O'Connor of Shelbourne still holds the all-time record of two minutes 14 seconds, which he established against Bohemians in 1967.

The English League record of two minutes 30 seconds Hayter broke was shared by Jimmy Scarth of Gillingham (against Leyton Orient, 1952) and Ephraim Dodds of Blackpool (against Tranmere, 1943).

BELOW Argentina's Batistuta (Number 9) wheels away after the first goal of his hat-trick against Greece, World Cup 1994

Half-time

HALF-TIME IS THE PERIOD WHEN managers can re-motivate teams, teacups can be thrown and substitutions planned. For the spectator, it's a chance to be fed and watered, which in practice often means joining the loo and/or burger-bar queue. The length of the interval seems to have increased from ten to 15 minutes by stealth: a FIFA meeting in 2004 debated but then rejected a German motion to further increase this to 20 minutes, studies in that country having shown that a five-minute extension would mean an increase of at least £200,000 a year per club in food and drink takings.

Almost every ground in Britain features some form of timepiece to count down the 45-minute halves; the most famous is the Clock End at Highbury. These days, however, the time is usually displayed digitally. Half-time scoreboards appear, by and large, to be a thing of the past. Jumbo TV-style screens now offer not only scores but highlights of previous games, advertisements and messages. Half-time entertainment can include penalty shootouts or schoolboy games, dance troupes, club mascots or even musical acts.

Perhaps the biggest innovation, however, is the advent of half-time betting. When Manchester City came back from 3-0 down at Tottenham to win 4-3 in early 2004, a gambler – who wasn't even a City fan – won a reported six figure sum backing them to win the Cup tie by that exact score. He certainly had a better outcome than the fan who left the ground…

RIGHT Manchester City and Spurs contest a match that saw the Light Blues turn round a 3-0 half-time deficit

Internationals

WE HAVE CHARLES ALCOCK, secretary of the FA between 1870 and 1896, to thank for the FA Cup and inter-national matches. He proposed the for-mer, based on the inter-house knockout competitions he had observed whilst at school at Harrow, in 1871, and the FA Cup has gone on to become perhaps the best known cup competition of all. He proposed the latter a year earlier, in 1870, and took part himself in the first, albeit unofficial match between England and Scotland that was played at Kennington Oval in March 1870 and ended all square at 1-1. There were to be a further four unofficial England and Scotland clashes, all played at Kennington Oval, although all of the players involved were based in London and Arthur Kinnaird (later Lord Kinnaird) turned out for Scotland in at least one of these clashes.

It was Alcock's desire to see Scottish players further afield interested in his proposal that led him to advertise for players in the Glasgow Herald in November 1870.

Although Queen's Park, the leading Scottish side of the day, read the letter with interest and sent former player Robert Smith as an observer, it was to take a further two years before England finally met Scotland in anything approaching an official capacity. Queen's Park entered the very first FA Cup competition, were exempt (on the grounds of travelling difficulties) until the semi-final and held Wanderers to a creditable draw. They were unable to afford to travel down again for the replay and therefore withdrew, but had in the meantime contacted Wanderers secretary Charles William Alcock and suggested that they could organise a

ABOVE A scroll commemorating the work of Charles Alcock, the father of international football

proper England-Scotland fixture.

As the Scottish Football Association was not formed until 1873, Queen's Park were seen as the 'establishment' in Scotland and their offer was eagerly taken up by Charles Alcock. Further, Queen's Park offered to guarantee the expenses of the travelling England side, and so on 30th November 1872, at the West of Scotland Cricket Club at Hamilton Crescent England and Scotland met in the very first international match.

The England-Scotland clash was the only international until 1879 when England met Wales for the first time and 1882 when they travelled to Belfast to meet Ireland. With regular fixtures in place, a British Championship was introduced in 1884 and survived for 88 seasons until it was abandoned in 1984. The success, however, of the competition was noted with interest overseas and in 1904 Belgium and France met at Uccle, near Brussels in the first international match ever to be played outside Great Britain.

Four years later England played their first overseas international matches, beating Austria 6-1 and 11-1, Hungary 7-0 and Bohemia 4-0 during the course of a week-long continental tour. By the 1920s virtually every country had played an international match and interest in the game worldwide was such that there were calls for an international competition. By 1930 this became reality with the creation of the World Cup.

It was NL Jackson, founder of amateur side The Corinthians, that first suggested the awarding of 'caps' in 1886 (players often wore them whilst playing in this era) and the first awarded were royal blue in colour with a rose on the front. Each player is given one cap per season, on to which is embroidered the initial letter of the country he has played against during that campaign.

BELOW Despite the lack of headgear, Alan Shearer and England boss Kevin Keegan are celebrating cap number 50 for the striker

Ireland

THE ENGLAND AND IRELAND clash in Belfast in 1882 was Ireland's very first international match, but the rest of the day went downhill; Oliver Vaughton and Arthur Brown became the first English players to register hat-tricks (Vaughton ended the match with five goals, Brown four) as England won 13-0!

Despite this unfortunate start Ireland eagerly accepted an invitation to take part in the British International Championship when it was launched in 1884. To begin with the Irish made up the numbers; they didn't beat the Welsh until 1887, the Scottish until 1899 and had to wait until 1913 before they finally got the better of the English!

With the creation of the Republic of Ireland in 1926, it was Northern Ireland who continued to compete in the British championship. To all intents and purposes, the rest of the Home Countries ignored the Republic, at least football-wise, with England not playing them until 1946, Wales until 1960 and Scotland until 1961. Even more surprisingly, Northern Ireland and the Republic of Ireland have met in only one friendly international since 1926, in 1999, although they have been drawn in the same qualifying groups for either the European Championships or World

BELOW Keane as mustard! Robbie celebrates a World Cup penalty, 2002

Cup four times. Even when the Republic did create a little bit of history, the 'rules' were changed: they were the first overseas country to beat England on home soil, registering a 2-0 win at Everton in 1949, but most record books tend to overlook this reverse.

Whilst Northern Ireland's greatest moments on the world stage were in the 1958 and 1982 World Cups, when they qualified from the group stage, the Republic had to wait longer before making an impact. The appointment of former England international Jack Charlton galvanised the country and helped the Republic qualify for the 1990 World Cup finals in Italy.

Charlton worked a miracle again in getting the side to the finals of the European Championships in 1992 and the World Cup in 1994. His successor Mick McCarthy did equally well to qualify for the final tournament in Japan and Korea in 2002.

Invariably calls for a united Irish side have grown in volume over the years. Certainly, the thought of a side that can combine the collective talents of Robbie Keane, Roy Keane, Matt Holland, Keith Gillespie and Damien Duff would take some beating.

Italy

FOUNDED IN 1898, THE ITALIAN football association is one of Europe's oldest and, with three World Cup wins and a European Championship victory, one of its most successful. For the last 40 or so years, Italy has also been the home of some of the most successful European club sides, seeing Juventus and both Milan clubs, AC and Inter, triumph in the European Cup.

Hosts for the very first World Cup tournament played in Europe in 1934, the Italian side was somewhat hijacked by the political aspirations of dictator Benito Mussolini. If Italy were to stage the World Cup, then they had to win it. To this end three Argentinean-born players were made into naturalised Italians, with Raimondo Orsi going on to net in the Final.

Italy's passage to the Final was not all plain sailing, having to overcome Greece in a qualifier and being involved in a violent clash with the Spaniards in the quarter-final that required a replay before Italy finally won 1-0. They fell behind in the Final against Czechoslovakia, were forced to switch their forwards around in a desperate bid to get on terms and finally won the match in extra time.

Four years later Italy became the first side to successfully defend their world title. Although only two of the 1934 side retained their place in the 1938 team, a fair few had helped Italy win gold at the 1936 Olympic games.

Not for the last time, Brazil were the pre-tournament favourites, and so confident were they of winning the trophy they left two of their better players, Leonidas and Tim, out of the semi-final against Italy in order to rest them for the Final. In the event the Italians won 2-1 and then beat Hungary 4-2 in an exciting match.

The outbreak of the Second World War brought international football to a standstill, but it is worth recording that for the duration of the war Ottorino Barassi, the secretary of the Italian FA, kept the Jules Rimet trophy in safe-keeping in a shoe box hidden under his bed!

Despite producing some enterprising sides after the war had ended, most notably Torino in the late 1940s, Italian football for the next 30 or so years became remembered for its negativity. Despite luring goalscorers of the calibre of Jimmy Greaves, Denis Law and later Ian Rush with the promise of huge salaries, Italian football was seldom exciting even if it was successful.

A disastrous World Cup in 1966, when they were eliminated in the group stages by North Korea (the Italian team were pelted with rotten fruit when they arrived home!) was followed by a better showing in 1970 in Mexico. After qualifying from their group with one victory, two draws and just a single goal, they

BELOW Italy suffers World Cup humiliation in 1966 as North Korea's Pak Doo Ik nets

opened up a little in the quarter-finals, beating the host nation 4-1.

Italy then played their part in one of the most thrilling World Cup matches of all time in overcoming the West Germans 4-3 in the semi-final, but in the Final the mighty Brazilians ran out easy 4-1 victors.

Eliminated early on in 1974, Italy finished fourth in 1978 and were fortunate to qualify out of their group in 1982, drawing all three of their matches. Thereafter, Italy got better as the competition progressed, winning both their second stage group matches, against world champions Argentina and a thrilling encounter with favourites Brazil, and then Poland in the semi-finals. Whilst the Final against West Germany was not a showpiece, Italy proved well worth the 3-1 victory.

Their best show-

ing since then has been the 1994 tournament in the US, where Italy were unfortunate to lose on penalties in the Final to the Brazilians.

More importantly, the reliance on defence and hitting sides on the break has changed. Although it is still not possible to describe the Italians as carefree or attack-minded as the Brazilians, the game in Italy is an altogether more entertaining prospect than it was 20 years ago.

RIGHT Sadly, Baggio's penalty shoot-out failure in 1994 saw Brazil take the World Cup

Keepers

ENGLAND HAS PRODUCED SOME excellent goalkeepers down the years, the finest of whom was probably Gordon Banks. He played in 73 full internationals and, amongst his many memorable saves, was the one from Pelé in the 1970 World Cup. Neither Pelé, nor anybody else, could believe it when Banks tipped that particular shot over the bar.

Ray Clemence won 61 England caps, and would have played for his country more often had it not been for the emergence of Peter Shilton. Shilton won a total of 125 caps and also played in a remarkable 1,005 league games prior to his retirement in 1997. After Shilton came David Seaman, another fine keeper who was England's first-choice custodian until 2002.

Until the late 1980s it was quite unusual to see a foreign born goal-keeper or, for that matter, any other player, turning out for an English League side. Manchester City did however have an acrobatic and brave foreign keeper many years earlier. He was

ABOVE The incomparable Gordon Banks of Leicester, Stoke and England

Bernhardt Trautmann, a former German prisoner of war, who guarded City's net between 1949 and 1964. Trautmann is famous for having broken his neck in the 1956 FA Cup Final – and playing on. Today, at least half of the keepers playing regularly in the Premiership are of foreign origin. Chelsea's Carlo Cudicini is one of the best: born in Milan in 1973, he made just one Premiership appearance at the end of season 1999-2000 before going on to be their regular first choice keeper. Fulham's Dutch international Edwin Van der Sar did much to help his side to a respectable place in the table in 2003-04, while Finnish keeper Antti Niemi (nicknamed 'Auntie' at St. Mary's), although somewhat injury-prone, has done well for Southampton. Three Americans – Brad Friedel (Blackburn Rovers), Tim Howard (Manchester United) and Kasey Keller (Tottenham Hotspur), have also made their mark as Premiership custodians.

The position of England's Number One is currently up for grabs. David James of Manchester City was in possession in early 2004; Tottenham's Paul Robinson was second choice, whilst Norwich City's 24-year-old keeper Robert Green is one to watch.

Kit

AS BRITAIN HAD BEEN THE HOME of football, most of the early kit manufacturers came from that territory. A glance at any early programme will reveal, apparel that is totally alien to today's streamlined kits.

The first major kit manufacturer in the UK was Umbro, a company set up by brothers Wallace and Harold Humphreys in Wilmslow in Cheshire in 1924. Within ten years Umbro had moved into supplying professional clubs, kitting out FA Cup winners Manchester City in 1934 and Sheffield Wednesday a year later. Umbro's influence extended beyond these shores and they were suppliers to the great Brazilian sides of 1958, 1962 and 1970. In 1966 Umbro supplied 15 of the 16 qualifiers for the World Cup finals in England, including hosts and winners England.

A year after Umbro first opened for business, German Adolf Dassler began making athletic shoes. He called his company Adidas, Adi being his family nickname and 'das' the first three letters of his surname. He chose three stripes

LEFT The old-fashioned football boot with nailed-in studs

as his company logo because that was how many sons he had. Whilst Adidas is still the largest supplier of athletic shoes in the world, it is with football kit that their reputation has been made. Adi's brother Rudolf also moved into kit manufacture following a disagreement with his brother and launched the Puma company, another major player in the market.

The most important development in recent years has been the arrival of the American company Nike. Formed in 1971 by Phil Knight and Jeff Johnson, the company can trace its roots back a further ten years when Knight and Bill

Bowerman had been importers of Japanese sports equipment into the American market. Their success as importers prompted them to go into manufacturing, and within ten years Nike was the predominant brand in the US. The distinctive 'swoosh', the brainchild of Caroline Davidson, depicts the wing of the Greek goddess of victory Nike from which the company got their name.

Just before the opening of the 1994 World Cup finals in America, Nike signed a sponsorship deal with the Brazilian football federation which prompted a number of other countries to sign up with them.

Players and former players have become increasingly involved in the design of boots, with Craig Johnston, the former Liverpool and Australia player, being responsible for the Predator boot.

Manufactured by Adidas and worn by current England captain David Beckham, the Predator has become the most popular football boot of the current age. With 'blades' instead of studs and a hefty pricetag, it typifies both the refinement and rewards associated with today's kit.

OPPOSITE KK is OK! Keegan celebrates a goal for England against Brazil, 1978

OPPOSITE BELOW Still smiling two decades later as national coach before his dramatic departure

BELOW Liverpool's Steven Gerrard proudly displays his blade-equipped Predators

Keegan

BORN IN ARMTHORPE, DONCASTER, on 14th February 1951, Joseph Kevin Keegan began his professional career with Scunthorpe United. A sharp and creative goalscorer, he was soon spotted by Bill Shankly, who secured his signature for Liverpool in 1971 for a bargain-basement fee of £35,000. Keegan went on to make 321 appearances for Liverpool, scoring on 100 occasions.

In June 1977, he moved to SV Hamburg, and later played for both Southampton and Newcastle. In-between times, he gained a host of domestic honours and played in European and UEFA Cup Finals. On the international front, he played for England 63 times.

Kevin Keegan the player was the footballing hero of his day. Unlike George Best, he coped well with the pressures and the dodgy fashion statements, and it was not surprising that, eventually, he went into management. After his retirement as a player in 1984, management was however put on hold. Keegan went to live in Spain for a number of years and did not return to this country until

February 1992. He then took over as Newcastle United, helping them avoid the drop into the old Division Three and then, in the following season, guiding them to the championship of the new Division One and promotion to the Premier League.

Having established himself as a Tyneside folk hero, Keegan quit Newcastle in 1996 after his side gave away a 13-point lead and lost out to Manchester United in the race for the Premiership title. He later joined Fulham as Chief Operating Officer with fellow former England man Ray Wilkins as his team manager.

Keegan enjoyed further success at Fayed's Fulham, especially when he later took direct control of the side. England however was expecting, and his tenure was to be a short one. Mohamed Fayed eventually, and most graciously, allowed his manager to leave Craven Cottage to take over as England manager. That post proved also to be very short-term as, following England's defeat by Germany in a Euro 2000 qualifying game, Keegan resigned – admitting, in effect, that he wasn't up to the job.

Kevin Keegan now manages Manchester City.

Le Tissier

MATTHEW LE TISSIER WAS AN enigma. One of the most gifted players to pull on an England shirt in the last few decades, he did so all too rarely. His cause might have been helped by a higher profile but, instead of transferring to a top club, the winger remained at his first love, Southampton. And in scoring the very last goal at the Dell before hanging up his boots in 2001, he cemented his position as that club's most famous and revered player of all time.

Born in the Channel Islands on 14th October 1968, Le Tissier became the first-ever man from Guernsey to play for the Saints when he made his debut as a substitute at Norwich in August 1986. Over the following years he turned in some brilliant displays, collecting the PFA Young Player of the Year award in 1990, and reached the

peak of his powers in the early 1990s. His best season was probably 1994-95 when he scored 30 goals, although the club finished only 10th.

This form saw him force his way into the England line-up but, never given a decent run in the side by Terry Venables, Le Tissier's club form suffered in 1995-96. He made a better start the following season and new national coach Glenn Hoddle included him in his World Cup squads. He was restored to the team against Italy, but was substituted in the second half. He would win a total of just eight full caps.

Although he attracted interest from bigger clubs over the years, Le Tissier was happy to stay with Southampton for whom he scored many brilliant and memorable goals. He had the additional ability to play a defence-splitting pass and curl a free-kick into the top corner.

Le Tissier played 431 League games for Southampton, 50 League Cup games and 32 FA Cup games. He scored 208 goals for the club, including an amazing 49 out of 50 penalties.

Liverpool

LIVERPOOL FOOTBALL CLUB was founded on 15th March 1892. Anfield has been the club's only home, but Everton originally played there before moving to Goodison Park. Liverpool first won the League Championship in 1901, and they have won it 18 times in all.

The club's most famous manager was undoubtedly the remarkable Bill Shankly. He took over at Anfield in December 1959 and remained in charge for almost 15 years. Liverpool were in the old Second Division when Shankly, a former Scotland international wing-half, joined them from Huddersfield Town, but they went on to become a very good side indeed. Bill Shankly was sometimes criticised for not bringing on enough home-grown youngsters, but amongst his most important sign-

ings were two players from Scunthorpe United – Kevin Keegan and goalkeeper Ray Clemence. The foundations were laid for the most exciting time in Liverpool's history.

When Shankly resigned, he was replaced by his assistant, the equally remarkable Bob Paisley. During Paisley's nine-year tenure, Liverpool won the League Championship six times, the European Cup three times, and the UEFA Cup once. They also won

BELOW Champagne days for Michael Owen like the 2003 League Cup win have been fewer and farther between than he and his Liverpool colleagues would have liked

the League Cup three times although the FA Cup eluded them. The club had continued success under Joe Fagan and Kenny Dalglish, but their supremacy did not last for ever.

Two tragedies had a serious effect on the club and on its supporters. In May 1985, 39 Italian fans died when a wall collapsed at the Heysel Stadium in Belgium, whilst Liverpool were playing Juventus in the European Cup Final. This led to Liverpool being banned from European competition for a decade but then, just four years later, 97 Liverpool supporters were killed in the Hillsborough disaster during an FA Cup semi-final against Nottingham Forest – a tragedy which changed the face of English football.

In recent years, as far as domestic and European honours are concerned, Liverpool have largely lost out to Manchester United and Arsenal. A joint management arrangement pairing Anfield veteran Roy Evans and French coach Gerard Houillier failed to spark, Houllier taking sole control in 1998. Players like Michael Owen and Harry Kewell seem to have gone off the boil of late but, in all probability, Liverpool will be back.

RIGHT Alan Kennedy kisses the European Cup, Liverpool's personal property in the late 1970s and early 1980s

Lineker

GARY WINSTON LINEKER, LEICESTER'S most famous crisp muncher, was born in that city on 30th November 1960 – his second name reflecting the fact that he was born on Churchill's birthday. Whilst at school, young Gary was an accomplished all round sportsman and, in a report, one of his teachers wrote: "He must devote less time to sport if he wants to be a success." The teacher got it wrong.

Lineker joined Leicester City and went on to play 209 games and score 103 goals. He then transferred to Everton where, in the short time he was at Goodison, he made 57 appearances, scoring on 40 occasions. His next stop was Barcelona, where he became a fluent Spanish speaker, scored 48 goals in 111 matches, won a Spanish Cup Winner's medal and a Spanish League Championship medal, and, in 1989, helped his side to win the European Cup Winners Cup. Returning to England later that year, he joined Tottenham Hotspur and went on to net 80 times in 138 games. He finished his career in Japan with Nagoya Grampus Eight, where he suffered continuously with a sore toe.

Gary Lineker played 80 times for England, and scored 48 goals – a record only bettered by Bobby Charlton. He captained the England side between 1990 and 1992. As well as being a prolific goalscorer, Lineker was a fine team player who prided himself on his

excellent disciplinary record. When he finished playing, he entered the world of the media, at first on radio and later on television.

He proved to be as good at broadcasting as he is at everything else – and he has never minded people having a gentle go at him about his sore toe or his exceptionally large ears. Famed for his advertising of Walkers Crisps, Gary Lineker led a consortium which was formed to take over the ailing Leicester City. The club now plays at the Walkers Stadium.

BELOW Gary Lineker evades Scotland's Alex McLeish in 1988 during one of his 80 games for England

Matthews

STANLEY MATTHEWS WAS BORN in Hanley, one of Stoke's five towns, on 1st February 1915. He was the son of a professional boxer and he joined Stoke City as an outside-right in 1932. From

the beginning, Matthews was an outstanding player. His body swerve and ball control became famous, and he was eventually to become known as the Wizard of the Dribble. Full-backs didn't stand a chance as Stanley ghosted past them and then proceeded to cross the ball with pin-point accuracy.

Matthews had been a schoolboy international, and he went on to play 54 times for England at senior level. He would have won many more caps today, but there were fewer international matches played in those days, and in any case the war intervened. In 1947, having played in 259 League games for Stoke, he moved to Blackpool for what now seems a paltry fee

of £11,500. He had scored 51 League goals for his home town club, but he had made many more. Matthews was to remain at Blackpool until 1961 when, at the age of 46, he went back to Stoke to see out his playing days, and help regain top division status.

The highlight of Stanley Matthews' outstanding career had undoubtedly been what became known as the Matthews Final. In 1953, Blackpool faced Bolton Wanderers at Wembley. It was probably Matthews' last chance of an FA Cup winner's medal, but at one stage his team was 3-1 down. Blackpool recovered to win 4-3, with Stanley Matthews creating two of their goals and Stan Mortensen scoring a hat-trick. Stanley M probably thought the game should have been called the Mortensen Final, but you can bet he didn't care.

Stanley Matthews, a modest man who liked a pint or three, continued playing past his 50th birthday. He never earned more than about £75 a week and he made his last appearance for Stoke City in 1965. In that same year, he became Sir Stanley. He died, aged 85, in the year 2000.

Moore

BOBBY MOORE WAS A natural wing-half. Born in Barking on 12th April 1941, Robert Frederick Chelsea Moore went on to play, not for Chelsea, but for West Ham United. He made 642 appearances for the east London club

LEFT Bobby Moore pictured as captain of West Ham, first of his two London clubs

between 1958 and 1974, during which time he became one of the finest players this country has ever known. Towards the end of his career he played 150 times for Fulham.

Bobby Moore's West Ham won the FA Cup in 1964, and went on to lift the European Cup Winners' Cup a year later. Moore was to visit Wembley again in 1975 when, as a Fulham player, he faced his old club in another FA Cup final, but this time he was to finish on the losing side. It was however on the international scene that Moore was to make the greatest impression. He played for England on 108 occasions, and he was captain for 90 of those games – equalling the record set by Billy Wright.

Moore was not the quickest defender in the world but he always seemed to have time to spare when on the ball, and he fitted beautifully into England manager Alf Ramsey's 4-2-4 formation. The highlight of his career came in July 1966, when he shook hands with the Queen (having first wiped his muddy hands on the silk covering of the Royal Box) and then lifted the World Cup for the whole of England to admire.

During the run-up to the 1970 World Cup finals, Bobby Moore was accused by the police in Bogota, Columbia of stealing a gold bracelet from a hotel shop. He was later cleared but, whilst still under suspicion, he played the game of his life against Brazil. Although England lost this match, it will always be remembered for Gordon Banks' save and Moore's remarkable performance.

When he retired, Booby Moore had a go at management with Oxford United and Southend, but without great success. He died of cancer in 1993 at the tragically early age of 51 and, although he had long ago received the OBE, it was felt by many that he had not been sufficiently honoured during his lifetime.

Maradona

STRIKER DIEGO ARMANDO Maradona's career took him from Buenos Aires' slums to the captaincy of his country, leading Argentina to 3-2 victory over Germany in the World Cup Final of 1986. Sadly, like the similarly gifted George Best and Paul Gascoigne, the tale was to end in tragedy.

Having made his professional debut age 15 and taken his international bow a

His fortunes in four World Cups graphically illustrated his rise and fall. In 1982, he had been sent off in Spain for youthful frustration (though his £1.7 million transfer to Barcelona followed), while eight years later in Italy he again managed to steer his country to the Final. But an early exit from the 1994 tournament followed a positive drugs test and his team flopped in the absence of their talismanic captain.

Leaving Italy in 1991, the year he failed his first drugs test, Maradona returned home via Seville and retired in 1997 on his 37th birthday shortly after a third drugs bust. Three years later he went to Cuba in an attempt to recover his health.

In 2004 he was admitted to a private clinic in Buenos Aires in a critical condition, suffering high blood pressure and respiratory failure. The 43-year-old, still feted as a national hero despite his misdemeanours, had been watching former side Boca Juniors play.

Four years earlier, Maradona had tied with Pelé for the accolade of FIFA's best ever player, he has had a musical written about the his rags-to-riches life and, despite his problems, boasts a 20,000-strong worldwide fan club.

mere six months later, Maradona left Boca Juniors for Spanish giants Barcelona in 1982. There his ankle was badly broken and, it's believed, he sought solace in drugs for the first time. He joined Napoli in 1984 for a then world record £4.1 million, transforming a mediocre team and leading them to two Championships and the UEFA Cup amid much hero-worship from their hard-core 'tifosi' fans.

Together with the Mexico World Cup, where he scored the infamous 'Hand of God' goal against England en route to Final victory, this was undoubtedly the period when Maradona played his finest football.

ABOVE Argentina's Diego Maradona as he should be remembered, in his playing prime

Newcastle

MANY OF THE MOST DEDICATED football fans in the world are to be found in the north-east of England, and a lot of these support Newcastle United. Long before the majority of supporters were to be seen wearing over-priced replica gear, the terraces and stands of St James' Park were adorned with thousands of men, women and children in Magpie striped shirts.

RIGHT Skipper Bobby Moncur displays Newcastle's last major trophy, the Inter Cities' Fairs Cup, won in 1969

Newcastle United was formed in 1892, following the merger of several local clubs. Throughout its proud history, the club has won the League Championship four times, and the FA Cup on six occasions. In recent times however, the record has not been quite so impressive. Newcastle last won the League Championship in 1927. During part of the 1980s, and again during the early 1990s, they were out of the top division and, although they were Premiership runners-up in 1996 and 1997 and FA Cup runners-up in 1974, 1998 and 1999, their last major honour was the Inter Cities' Fairs Cup in 1969.

This really isn't good enough for the fans, but they certainly admire and respect their remarkable manager, Sir Bobby Robson. Sir Bobby who, as a player, won 20 caps for England and who had previously managed Vancouver Whitecaps, Fulham, Ipswich,

PSV Eindhoven, Sporting Lisbon, FC Porto and Barcelona – as well as England – took over at Newcastle in September 1999. Famous for getting people's names wrong and for quotes such as: "We didn't underestimate them. They were a lot better than we thought," Sir Bobby is nevertheless an astute manager with unbounded energy and a deep love of the game. Now 71, he is still determined to achieve yet more success on Tyneside. With players like Kieron Dyer, Jermaine Jenas, Gary Speed and the evergreen Alan Shearer to work with, who can say he won't achieve his goal?

Non-League

NON-LEAGUE FOOTBALL IN England has typically been played on an amateur or semi-professional basis, but in recent years full professionalism has become the norm in the Football Conference, the next rung of the ladder down from the 92 Premier and Football League clubs. This has been the result of a second promotion place being made available in 2003, this being decided by a play-off competition featuring the second, third, fourth and fifth teams (the Champions being promoted as of right). Prior to 1987, admission to the Football League was on a discretionary basis, leading more often than not to the 'old pals' act' where League chairmen voted to retain the clubs already in place.

There have been notable successes among the clubs which have graduated from non-League. Wimbledon, admitted in 1977 in place of Workington after 88 years of existence, were playing in the top flight within a decade (Workington, the team they replaced, never made it back), while Doncaster Rovers, who ascended in 2003, obtained successive promotions, underlining the parity between Third Division and Conference. Rushden and Diamonds,

ABOVE The eyes have it. Sir Bobby Robson observes from the dugout

formed from the amalgamation of two Northamptonshire clubs, made it to the League in 2001 funded by footwear magnate Max Griggs' millions.

The Non-League game has traditionally been organised on the basis of a so-called pyramid system. The Football Conference is at the top of the Pyramid, which has a 1-3-5-15 structure with 205 teams in the top 3 steps. The end of the 2003-04 season saw a major restructuring operation take place in the leagues below the Football Conference. This took the shape of a 1-2-3-4-15 structure, two 22-club Conference North and South divisions being inserted between the Conference proper and the Isthmian League, Southern League and Northern Premier League which had up until then supplied the three teams to enter the Conference.

Within a few seasons the one-time pyramid will have mutated further into a 1-2-3-4-12 structure as the 15 'step 5' leagues reduce to 12. There will be 220 teams in the top 4 steps, so 15 teams will move up from the new step 5. There will be no direct links between leagues for promoted and relegated teams; instead, boundaries will be drawn on a geographical basis once promoted and relegated teams are known each season.

Nicknames

WHO DO YOU SUPPORT? THE Spireites, Cobblers, Rams or Bantams? Fans of Chesterfield, Northampton, Derby County and Bradford City know who we're talking about – we are, of course, talking nicknames.

Most tend to stick – hence Fulham will always be the Cottagers wherever they end up playing on a permanent basis. Similarly Sheffield Wednesday's 'Owls' appellation results from their Hillsborough ground being known as Owlerton until 1912. Bristol Rovers' Eastville home, which they left in 1986, was next to a gasworks, a fact mocked by Bristol City fans but taken up as a badge of pride by Rovers' Gasheads. (The official nickname of the club was and remains the Pirates.)

Some labels like Liverpool's 'Reds' or Tottenham Hotspurs' 'Spurs' are mundane. More original nicknames resulting from the club colours include the Canaries of Norwich with their bright yellow shirts and Queens Park Rangers, traditionally the Rs, who have recently become the Super Hoops due to their blue and white hooped jerseys. There's a

striped Everton Mint, and the club are known as the Toffees, but their shirts remain deepest blue.

Tradition plays a major part. West Bromwich Albion was formed as a works team for the local iron works where the foundry workers' trousers were known as Baggies. But the origins can get lost with the passage of time. Charlton's Addicks appellation comes either from the haddock which the team loved eating or the fact that, with commendable hospitality, they took their opponents for a fish supper after games. Take your pick – or you can just call them the Valiants!

Nicknames can change: Reading were known as the Biscuitmen but, after biscuit-making in the area declined in the 1970s, Royals was chosen as its replacement – perhaps because Berkshire is where Windsor Castle is situated.

Once the Rokerites, Sunderland became the Black Cats after a competition that coincided with their departure from Roker Park in 1997. Newcastle fans call them the Mackems, a term of abuse deriving from the days when Sunderland was a leading shipbuilding town. During the day, it's said, the shipbuilders built the ships, and during the night they would indulge in a little light-fingered 'piracy'.

Using the dialect of the time, people – no doubt from Newcastle – said of the Sunderland men, "They maak 'em then taak 'em" (make them then take them). Somehow, the first part has stuck! Similarly Portsmouth fans call their Southampton neighbours Scummers after Southampton dock workers apparently broke a strike.

Perhaps the nicest nickname source is Bury's Shakers. When asked about his team's chances against mighty Blackburn Rovers in the 1892 Lancashire Cup Final, club chairman JT Ingham was reported to have said, "We'll shake 'em!"

They did, 2-0!

BELOW Shakers in more ways than one! Bury celebrate promotion as Division Two champs in 1997

Okocha

BORN ON 14TH AUGUST 1973 IN Enugu, Nigeria, Augustine Jay Jay Okocha first began playing at the age of three and signed for local Rangers International at the age of 16. It was on holiday in Germany that his skills first attracted wider interest and he initially signed with Borussia Neunkirchen of the German Fourth Division. In 1992 he made the leap into the top flight with Eintracht Frankfurt. Here he was an instant crowd favourite, delighting all and sundry (if not the opposition) with his flicks and trickery.

In the space of four seasons Jay Jay made 90 appearances for the German side, scoring 17 goals and also began his full international career (he currently has more than 60 caps), helping Nigeria to win Olympic gold in the 1996 football tournament and the African Nations Cup in 1998.

By then Okocha had swapped the cold climate of Germany for warmer temperatures in Turkey, signing for Fenerbahce in 1996 in a deal that cost the Turkish club £1 million. They got an immediate return on their investment, for at the end of his first season with the club they had lifted the Turkish League title. Okocha spent two years in Turkey, making 63 appearances and scoring a more than healthy return of 30 goals. Then an astonishing £10 million transfer took him to France and Paris St Germain, easily the most expensive deal involving a Nigerian player.

Goals were not so easy to come by in the French League, and Okocha's 83 appearances

BELOW Bolton and Nigeria's inspiration in Premiership action against Manchester City, April 2004

in four seasons saw only 12. Unable to find a buyer prepared to pay their inflated transfer fee, Paris St Germain were finally to lose Okocha's services on a free transfer at the end of the 2001-02 season. Impressive performances during the World Cup finals in Japan and South Korea alerted a number of Europe's top clubs as to his availability, but by then Okocha had already reached agreement with Sam Allardyce and Bolton Wanderers for his services. It was a quite astonishing coup and, galvanised by their inspirational talisman, Bolton staved off relegation and looked a better unit by the time the 2003-04 season opened. Jay Jay Okocha hadn't finished there either, helping the club reach the Final of the Carling Cup against Middlesbrough.

His ball control and dribbling, his audacity in attempting crossfield passes and permanent smile have made him an almost permanent fixture on (Sky TV) Soccer AM's slot devoted to trickery, but as defences up and down the country will attest, there is more to Okocha's game than fancy flicks. To Bolton fans' discomfiture, however, there are a host of clubs lining up to try and lure him into their current formations.

Owners

WHEN FOOTBALL WAS IN ITS infancy, all manner of businessmen got attracted into funding a club. Invariably there were sound business reasons for so doing; John Houlding had invested in Everton in order to provide thirsty customers for his premises near their ground at Anfield, Sandon Hotel. Similarly, Spurs move into White Hart Lane was assisted by the brewers Charrington who had noticed great takings at public houses near football grounds.

As football grew, the directors saw their role in a different light. Now, being a member of the board at a successful club was seen as something of a status symbol.

Perhaps the most famous football dynasty in England had been the Edwards family at Manchester United, with butcher Louis Edwards passing on control of the club to his son Martin. Similarly, the Agnelli family in Turin had bought into Juventus in the 1920s, a connection they retain to this day. A successful Juventus side, and they've had plenty of those over the years, ensures a happy workforce at the Fiat plant come Monday and increased production.

Buying into a football club doesn't always have to break the bank. Ken Bates bought control of Chelsea, after previously being involved with Oldham Athletic, for just £1, but he did have to guarantee their considerable debts into the bargain! While Bates developed Stamford Bridge into Chelsea Village, others have built new grounds, for example John Madejski (Reading), Dave Whelan (Wigan's JJB Stadium) and Firoz Kassam (Oxford).

It was Spurs who first came up with the idea of floating a club on the Stock Exchange as a means of raising revenue. Their reasoning at the time, back in 1983, was that just about every other industry, including a fair few from the entertainment sector, was listed on the Stock Exchange, so why not football clubs? At first the scheme was a success; the flotation was over-subscribed, a number of institutional investors had picked up shares and there were dividends paid for each of the next seven or so years.

But football is not like most other businesses. A club's fortunes off the field are almost directly linked to its fortunes on it. A bad run of results will drive some of the floating supporters away, revenues will drop and profits will fall. Whilst the fan will not contemplate selling his meagre shareholding, retaining it for sentimental reasons and to feel he owns a bit of the club, the institutional investors are in it purely for the return.

BELOW Former Chelsea owner Ken Bates makes a point to manager Claudio Ranieri. Both men, sadly, fell from favour on Abramovich's arrival

Ooh aah Cantona

DURING HIS LONG AND SUCCESSFUL career in management, Alex Ferguson has bought many exciting players. Of all the deals the Scot has done, none have turned out to be as important as the one he did in taking Eric Cantona across the M62 for £1 million in 1992.

Born in Marseille on 24th May 1966, Eric joined Auxerre in 1981 and made his debut in 1983. After completing his national service. Eric was loaned out to Second Division club Martigues to gain first-team experience. He returned to Auxerre and signed professional forms in 1986, soon after representing his country at Under 21 and full level. In June 1988 he was transferred to Olympique Marseille for £2.3 million, but the move soon turned sour, not least because Eric has never been afraid to speak his mind.

Unable to gain his place in the side once he had recovered from injury, he was sold to Nimes-Olympique for £1 million and was soon back into trouble with the authorities. Hauled before a disciplinary committee for throwing a ball at a referee, Cantona was given a one-month ban. When he then went up to each committee member in turn and told them they were all idiots, this was doubled! Eric Cantona announced his immediate retirement from the game in December 1991.

He was persuaded to give it one last go in England and came over to talk to Sheffield Wednesday. Wednesday were unwilling to sign him without a trial so he headed up the M1 to talk to Leeds United. Howard Wilkinson signed the player on the spot and Eric repaid him by helping Leeds United win the League title at the end of the 1991-92 season. The fans took him to their hearts, coming up with the 'Ooh Aah Cantona' chant and turning him into a cult hero.

His surprise departure across the Pennines to sign for Manchester United saw him become the first player to win consecutive League titles with different clubs. The following year United retained their title and won the FA Cup to boot, only the fourth Double of the modern era.

They should have repeated the feat again in 1995, but Cantona was an enforced absentee. Once again, it was

his temperament that had caused the problem; reacting to taunting from a section of the crowd during United's clash with Crystal Palace, he had leapt the barrier and kung fu-kicked the fan with the biggest mouth! A seven-month ban and £10,000 fine were handed out by the football authorities, whilst the legal system subsequently handed him a two-week jail term, later reduced to 120 hours' community service.

With Cantona back in the side in November 1995, Manchester United returned to winning ways, landing another Double at the end of the season. That Eric should have been the man responsible for scoring the only goal of the FA Cup Final against Liverpool was the icing on the cake. At the end of the season he was named Football Writers' Player of the Year.

Eric collected his fourth and final League title medal with United at the end of the 1996-97 season, meaning he had won League titles in five out of the previous six years. Not a bad return for a player who had initially announced his retirement in 1991! Eric announced it again at the end of the season, preferring to look for new interests to keep him occupied.

Pelé

RIGHT The legendary
Pelé makes the draw
for the 2006 World Cup
qualifying rounds

WIDELY REGARDED AS THE FINEST player in the world, Edson Arantes do Nascimento, or Pelé as he is better known, was born in Tre Coracoes, Brazil on 23rd October 1940. The son of a professional footballer, Pelé was spotted at the age of 13 as a potential star for the future and guided through Santos' youth team to senior status, making his debut at the age of 16. He was not yet 17 when he made his debut for Brazil. A knee injury shortly before the World Cup squad left for Sweden in 1958 threatened to keep him home, but he recovered sufficiently to play in four of Brazil's six games. He scored six goals in the tournament, including two in the Final itself against Sweden.

The next two tournaments were personal disasters for Pelé; injured in the second game in 1962 he took no further part, although Brazil retained their trophy, and in 1966 brutal tackling by the Bulgarians and Portuguese saw both Pelé and Brazil off. He reached his peak in 1970 in Mexico, displaying alertness and skill levels never previously seen and scoring four times during the competition.

After retiring from the international scene in 1971 he spent three further years with Santos before heading to the United States and New York Cosmos, single-handedly popularising the game in the US. He retired for good in 1977, having played 1,363 matches and scored 1,281 goals, including 97 for Brazil. At a time when all of his compatriots were heading to Europe to make their fortunes, Pelé remained faithful to Santos, a decision that reinforced his reputation at home. On the world stage, he is equally revered, as evidenced by his honorary knighthood from Queen Elizabeth II in 1997 and the fact that he was coaxed out of retirement one final time in the early 1980s to play a starring role in the Michael Caine and Sylvester Stallone film Escape To Victory. Similar cameo appearances have seen him in Mike Bassett: England Manager and he is currently the face and voice of a worldwide Viagra campaign!

Premier League

THE INFLUX OF TELEVISION money into the game by the end of the 1980s had led many of the leading (for which you should read First Division) clubs to believe that they should receive a bigger share. Up until then the money was fairly evenly divided, with even the Fourth Division clubs, whose matches were seldom, if ever, shown live on television receiving a considerable sum.

By the turn of the decade, the leading clubs had had enough and 15 met at the FA's headquarters at Lancaster Gate in June 1991 to discuss the setting up of a Premier League under the control of the FA rather than the Football League. All agreed to resign from the Football League at

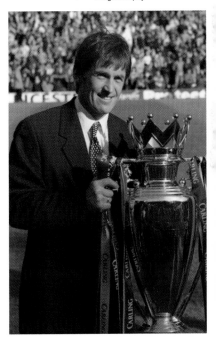

BELOW In 1995 Kenny Dalglish's Blackburn Rovers were the first team after two-time winners Manchester United to put their name on the Premier League trophy

the end of the season, with the rest of the First Division soon following suit. In January 1992 the FA council gave its seal of approval to a 22-team Premier League to commence season 1992-93, reducing to a 20-club division at the end of the 1994-95 season.

The new Premier League was able to offer, to the highest bidder, a flexible fixture schedule. One that would allow live matches to be played on a Sunday afternoon and Monday evening to begin with and, later on, matches played at 12 noon and 5.30pm on a Saturday.

With the Premier League awash with money (with the exception of Leeds United), there has been no shortage of world-class players eager to come and ply their trade in England, all well remunerated for their efforts. Thus the best that Croatia, Slovenia, Moldova and Bulgaria has to offer can be found alongside such stalwarts as Roy Keane, Duncan Ferguson, Ryan Giggs and others of their ilk from England's traditional hunting grounds of Ireland, Scotland and Wales. All the top players want to test their talents in the League described as the best in the world, but until Real and Athletico Madrid come calling the Premier League will do.

Penalties

AS HARD AS IT IS TO IMAGINE now, the early law-makers of the game did not include the provision of a penalty into their rules simply because they did not believe that anyone playing the game would try to do anything untoward to obtain an advantage, especially around the goal area. The launch of the FA Cup in 1872 and the Football League in 1888 soon changed all that!

It was perhaps the experiences of Stoke that led to the two most vital changes in the games' laws. In 1890, during an FA Cup quarter-final with Notts County, a goal-bound Stoke shot was punched away by a County defender with the result that Stoke were awarded a free kick on the County goal-line. The resulting kick was easily blocked and County went on to win the match.

Although the Irish FA had introduced the penalty kick in 1890, the English and Scottish FAs did not follow suit until the following year, no doubt influenced by reports from the Notts County and Stoke match. Stoke were to suffer again during that first season, for later on they were 2-1 down to Aston Villa late in the game when they were awarded a penalty and the chance to equalise.

A Villa player grabbed hold of the ball and booted it out of the stadium; by the time it was retrieved the referee had blown for full time! Not surprisingly, the laws were amended to allow time for a penalty to be taken.

History records that Alex McCall of Renton scored the very first penalty, against Leith Athletic in August 1891. Three weeks later John Heath of Wolverhampton Wanderers became the first player to score a penalty in an English game, netting in the 5-0 win over Accrington on 14th September.

It was Pelé who announced that a penalty was a cowardly way to score a goal (although it did not stop him netting the 1,000th goal of his professional career from

the penalty spot!) and there were those who held similar views; well-known amateur club Corinthian Casuals, according to legend, have never scored from the penalty spot in their long and distiguished history, deliberately missing every one since they believe in gentlemanly conduct.

BELOW Dave Beasant's 1989 FA Cup Final penalty save against Liverpool's John Aldridge that assured a Wimbledon victory

In the hundred years or so that have followed, the course of football history has been changed on the award of a penalty and the subsequent outcome of the resulting kick. Huddersfield Town became the first club to win the FA Cup thanks to a heatedly debated penalty award against Preston North End in 1927.

The same club had benefited three years earlier when a Cardiff City penalty against Birmingham City was saved, allowing Huddersfield to collect the League Championship, whilst both John Aldridge (for Liverpool against Wimbledon in 1989) and Gary Lineker (for Spurs against Nottingham Forest in 1991) saw their penalties in FA Cup finals at Wembley saved. Lineker suffered again the following year, for his penalty in a friendly international against Brazil was similarly saved.

It was the Watney Cup, a pre-season tournament of the early 1970s, that first experimented with the idea of a penalty shootout, whereby each side would take five penalties apiece at the end of a drawn game in order to decide the result. Since then the destiny of all of the major tournaments has been decided by the penalty shootout.

Queens Park Rangers

QUEENS PARK RANGERS FC CAME into being around 1886, when a team called St Jude's was amalgamated with a team called Christchurch Rangers. The club has had a number of homes including, for two short spells, London's White City Stadium, but its supporters have always preferred Loftus Road.

For many years in the shadow of more illustrious neighbours Chelsea and Fulham, the club finally gained Football League status with the formation of the Third Division in 1920. QPR remained a Third Division (South) club until, in 1948, they topped the division and won promotion to the Second.

Four years later they were relegated again, and they were to remain in Division Three until 1967.

The 1966-67 season was to prove a remarkable one for QPR. Not only did the team win the Third Division title,

BELOW Kevin Gallen and Marc Bircham celebrate a hair-raising goal, 2004

finishing 12 points clear of Middlesbrough, but they also won the first League Cup Final to be played at Wembley. On that memorable day they were 2-0 down at one stage, but they went on to beat West Bromwich Albion 3-2. Just over a year later they were playing in the (old) First Division, but Rangers were relegated after just one season in the top flight.

For some years after that they hovered between the top two divisions, but at the end of season 1975-76 manager Dave Sexton led his boys to second place in Division One – just one point behind League Champions Liverpool, and three points clear of Manchester United.

Since those heady days, the fortunes of Queens Park Rangers have ebbed and flowed. They were founder members of the Premiership in 1992, but financial problems and various other difficulties at Loftus Road have seen them slide slowly down the league. Sharing their ground with Fulham on a temporary basis helped on the financial front but the team still began 2003-04 in Division Two. As the season drew to a close, however, the happy reality of First Division football arrived once more in Shepherds Bush.

Queen's Park

THE STORY OF QUEEN'S PARK Football Club is one of the most remarkable in British football. Founded on the south side of Glasgow in 1867, Queen's Park was, for many years, Scotland's premier football club. Its directors were instrumental in the formation of the Scottish Football Association and, although it may now seem hard to believe, the club organised the first ever international between Scotland and England. That was in 1872, and every member of the Scotland side was a Queen's Park player.

As late as 1903, when Queen's Park played the inaugural match at their Hampden Park Stadium, the team was still a major force in Scottish football. That game, played before 44,530 spectators, resulted in a 1-0 win over local rivals Celtic. However, Queen's Park was a strictly amateur club and, by the turn of the century, professionalism had well and truly taken hold both north and south of the border. In one sense, the halcyon days were over, yet the club carried on into the Twentieth Century and is still playing Scottish League football more than a hundred years later.

As time went by, the fortunes of Queen's Park FC inevitably waned. This was largely due to the club's insistence on maintaining its amateur status but it continued to play an important role by grooming future professionals who later went on to play for other Scottish clubs. Perhaps the most remarkable thing of all is that Queen's Park continue to play at Hampden. Before the stadium was rebuilt during the 1990s, the club would play its league games with just a few hundred supporters standing on terraces which could accommodate upwards of 150,000 people. Hampden

ABOVE A contemporary depiction of Queen's Park's defeat in the 1884 English FA Cup Final against Blackburn Rovers

Park may be Scotland's national stadium, but the Scottish Football Association still has to lease it from a Third Division club – and an amateur one at that.

Quickest goals

AS A GOAL CAN'T BE SCORED direct from the kick-off, the feat of British non-League footballer Marc Burrows who, in April 2004, scored the world's fastest-ever goal in just two seconds, is unlikely ever to be beaten.

ABOVE Hakan Sukur edges ahead of opponent Hong Myung-bo en route to the World Cup's fastest ever goal, 2002

"My fellow striker Michael Pointer rolled the ball forward a couple of inches and I took a mighty swing at it. The wind was strong and the ball just sailed over their keeper. I was so stunned I didn't really celebrate. I put my arms in the air and burst out laughing." Burrows went on to score a hat-trick as Cowes Sports reserves beat Eastleigh reserves 5-3.

The former Portsmouth trainee added: "I've tried something similar but it normally goes out for a throw-in and I feel like a right prat." Manager Paul Sleep said: "Their goalkeeper was a little too far off his line. The poor lad looked shocked and amazed." Referee John Sorrell said it was the best goal he has ever seen. "It's difficult to see how a goal could possibly be scored quicker."

The record had previously been held by Uruguay's Ricardo Olivera, who scored in 2.8 seconds for Ro Negro against Soriano in 1998. Britain's previous fastest strike was timed out in 3.5 seconds by Colin Cowperthwaite in 1979 for Barrow against Kettering in the Conference. The honour of scoring the fastest Premiership goal is shared by Ledley King (Tottenham-Bradford City) and Alan Shearer (Newcastle-Manchester City) at just 10 seconds.

The fastest goal in World Cup history was scored by Hakan Sukur in just 11 seconds in June 2002 as Turkey beat co-hosts South Korea 3-2 to clinch third place. The 30-year-old Parma forward hadn't scored in Turkey's six previous matches and capitalised on rival skipper Hong Myung-bo's attempted pass back to slot a right-foot shot wide of the Korean keeper. He beat the previous record of 15 seconds held by Vaclav Masek since Czechoslovakia's first-round match against Mexico in 1962.

The first ever first-minute goal in the World Cup went to Emile Veinante of France in the 40th second of the match against Belgium in June 1938 in Paris. The fastest goal by a substitute went to Denmark's Ebbe Sand who scored in his first minute on the pitch against Nigeria in June 1998.

Rooney

MERSEYSIDE TEENAGER WAYNE Rooney has been compared with Paul Gascoigne for his precocious talents – but in reality his breakthrough to international fame was more similar to fellow Liverpool lad Michael Owen. Just as the previously little-known Owen starred in the 1998 World Cup, Rooney took the 2004 European Championships in Portugal by the scruff of the neck, scoring four goals in the group stages and, before he broke a bone in his foot in the quarter-final against the home nation, looked to be in the running for player of the tournament honours.

He'd graduated to the Everton first team in 2002 aged just 15 and was initially shielded from the limelight by manager David Moyes. But goals such as his 30-yard winner against Arsenal (and England goalkeeper David Seaman) in that October inevitably brought him to the attention of England manager Sven-Goran Eriksson and Rooney's international debut against Australia in 2003 made him the country's youngest ever full representative.

His first 15 England games brought seven goals, compared with Owen's five,

BELOW Wayne Rooney celebrates scoring against Switzerland Euro 2004

but it was his Euro 2004 brace against Croatia, following a previous pair against Switzerland, that marked him down as a world-class star – especially since the Croats had publicly targeted him for rough treatment. Rooney's volatile temperament was undoubtedly at odds with Owen's ice-cold demeanour on the pitch, but England team-mate Rio Ferdinand proclaimed him "more streetwise than Michael was six years ago". He would clearly need all that and more to keep his feet on the ground, with post-tournament headlines proclaiming a likely £50 million move to a top English club like Manchester United or Chelsea.

Cash-strapped Everton were unlikely to hang on to their star striker, no matter what their adoring fans might hope, but another successful season at Goodison Park could see Rooney take his pick of Europe's premier sides. At the end of only his second year as a professional footballer, the 18 year-old had the brightest future imaginable. And even if he lacked the looks and superstar partner of David Beckham (whose shirt was the star-struck teenager's most prized souvenir from Euro 2004), Wayne's world appeared to have no boundaries.

Ronaldo

WIDELY REGARDED AS THE MOST complete footballer of his generation, Ronaldo was born in Bento Ribeiro, a suburb of Rio De Janeiro on 22nd September 1976 and became a major star in a youth tournament in Colombia in 1992. He was subsequently signed by Cruzeiro di Belo Horizonte, collecting a $50,000 signing-on fee in the process.

Called up for the full Brazilian side at the age of 17, he was little more than a squad player for that World Cup however, but had already secured a move to PSV Eindhoven, joining the club in the summer of 1994.

He was an instant success at PSV, netting 30 goals in just 33 League appearances, but a knee injury halted his progress during his second season in Holland. In 1996 he signed with Barcelona for a £12 million transfer fee.

When Inter Milan made their move a year later, the fee had risen to £18 million. Whilst Ronaldo was unable to help Inter to the League title, he did play a leading part in the UEFA Cup that season as Inter beat Italian rivals Lazio 3-0 in the Final.

It was supposed to be the first course, with Brazil winning the 1998 World Cup in France the main course. But things didn't go according to plan. The night before the Final, Ronaldo was rushed to hospital after suffering from a fit. Although tests revealed nothing serious, Ronaldo was a mere shadow of his previous self as the French powered their way to an easy victory.

After rest and recuperation, Ronaldo returned to Inter and set about re-establishing his reputation. But injury blighted his time in Italy and he made just 36 appearances in three years (scoring 24 goals). He missed the entire 2000-01 season, and lingering doubts over his fitness left Inter open to offers for their star.

But Ronaldo let his football do the talking and was once again in demand after a successful 2002 World Cup when he scored both goals in the Final as Brazil reclaimed their world title.

Those golden goals alone prompted Real Madrid to pay £28.9 million to include Ronaldo in their team of all the talents. He has not disappointed either, netting 23 in his first season as Real Madrid won the League title. What lies ahead for this talented yet injury-prone footballer? Who knows – but at least he has the consolation of knowing that time is still on his side.

BELOW Ronaldo, the world's most famous centre-forward, in international action

RIGHT David Beckham was added to Madrid's star players or 'galacticos' in summer 2003

Real Madrid

A RECENT SURVEY of newspaper editors around the world asked who was the biggest football club in the world. The majority answered Real Madrid.

Formed as Madrid FC in the late 1890s by students, the club has its official birth given as March 1902. In 1920 the club was granted the prefix Real, meaning Royal, by King Alfonso XIII and became founder members of the Spanish League in 1927 and have never been relegated out of the First Division.

Real Madrid's elevation to worldwide recognition can be traced back to 1943 with the appointment of Santiago Bernabeu as club president. A former player, coach and secretary of the club, Bernabeu's vision and fundraising abili-

ties transformed the club on and off the pitch. He turned their ground at Chamartin from a crumbling relic that accommodated 14,000 in 1943 to a superb new stadium with room for 75,000 by 1949. During the 1950s, financed by European success, the Estadio Bernabeu could hold 125,000. Fans from across the country flocked to see some of the best players in the world

– Hungarian Ferenc Puskas, Argentinean Alfredo Di Stefano and homegrown stars such as Francsico Gento.

Whilst they are undoubtedly the most successful side at home, having won the League title 29 times (their nearest rivals Barcelona can only muster 16) and the cup 17 times (here Barcelona and Athletic Bilbao hold sway, having won 24 and 23 times respectively), it is their unrivalled European success that has made their name. Winners of the European Cup in each of its first five seasons, they found further success in 1966, 1998, 2000 and 2002. Added to this are victories in the UEFA Cup in 1985 and 1986, in the process becoming the first side to retain the trophy. The only European trophy to elude them was the European Cup' Winners Cup, but only just, for they were beaten finalists in 1971 and 1983.

In recent years Real Madrid has also grabbed back its reputation as the hirers of the best footballing talent in the world. The current side boasts such illustrious names as Zidane, Carlos, Figo, Raul and Ronaldo, alongside England captain David Beckham. If there is a player with abilities better than any on the squad of Real Madrid, then he will be targeted as a potential recruit before too long. The club formed by students and taken to undreamed-of heights by Santiago Bernabeu have no intention of giving up their title of the world's biggest club too lightly.

BELOW Real skipper Zarrago displays the European Cup after defeating Reims in the 1959 Final

Scotland

RIGHT Ally's Tartan Army followed their team to Argentina but not to glory in 1978

BELOW Former German manager Berti Vogts took charge of Scotland in January 2002, but found the going tough

SCOTTISH FOOTBALL HAS A LONG and varied history. From the early days, when Irish immigrants helped to build a stadium for Celtic Football Club at Parkhead, Glasgow, to the present day, with Celtic and Rangers dominant in the domestic league, the game has always held a fascination for the Scots.

In recent decades the dominance of Rangers and Celtic has meant that other sides can barely get a look-in, and this has caused problems for those other clubs – and for the league itself. Many of the smaller clubs have faced, or are facing, bankruptcy, and from time to time the call comes for the big two to join the English Premiership.

Rangers and Celtic would indeed bring extra spice to the English league, but their absence from Scottish football might actually cause more difficulties for the rest of Scotland as some very large 'gates' would be lost. The Scottish game has not always been dominated by the Old Firm. Both Heart of Midlothian and Hibernian, the Edinburgh equivalent of Glasgow's big two, have won the Scottish League title on several occasions, Aberdeen winning it as recently as

1980, and then again in 1984 and 1985. It remains to be seen whether or not any side will come along to rival the Glasgow clubs in the future.

On the international front, Scotland has often flattered to deceive. Many Scots blame the fact that, in the past, some of their best players plied their trade in England, and never seemed to play as well when they returned home for international appearances. Today, Rangers and Celtic employ large numbers of foreign players and this also probably damages the prospects for up-and-coming Scottish footballers. It seems likely that international success will continue to evade Scotland for the foreseeable future despite the efforts of their first foreign manager Berti Vogts.

Shearer

WHEN SOMEBODY PLACED A giant replica Alan Shearer shirt on Antony Gormley's statue The Angel of the North, nobody in Newcastle was in the least surprised. A true local hero, Shearer is still knocking them in on Tyneside and he is tipped as the mana-gerial successor to another legend, Sir Bobby Robson.

Alan Shearer was born in Newcastle on 13th August 1970, but he began his career with Southampton in 1987 before moving to Blackburn Rovers in the summer of 1992 for a £3.6 million fee. By the time he was transferred to Newcastle in 1996, having turned down a move to Manchester United, the fee

BELOW Evergreen Alan Shearer celebrates another successful strike against PSV Eindhoven in 2004

had risen to a then world record £15 million. In between times, Shearer had turned himself into a world-class goalscorer for club and country. In his 63 England appearances, he netted 30 times and everyone thought he would go on forever. In a sense, he has gone on forever, but not playing for England. Although he scored the winning goal against Germany, he struggled a little during Euro 2000 and then announced his international retirement.

Shearer probably made the right decision, although many would like to see him in the current England squad. A careful and, some would say, somewhat taciturn and boring character, his career has probably lasted longer than it would have done had he continued to play for his country, and he has been perfectly happy scoring goals for his beloved Newcastle over the last few years. Refreshingly, Alan Shearer tends to shun celebrity status. Undemonstrative in television interviews, and once described by England keeper (and former Blackburn colleague) Tim Flowers as 'Mogadon Man', Shearer is not everybody's idea of a sparkling personality. Good for him; he has always known what he was about.

Shilton

PETER LESLIE SHILTON WAS BORN in Leicester on 18th September 1949. He made his first appearance as Leicester City's goalkeeper during season 1965-66 and his last as Leyton Orient's keeper in 1996-97. He also played for Stoke City, Nottingham Forest, Southampton, Derby County, Plymouth Argyle and Bolton Wanderers. When he finally called it a day, he had made a quite stupendous 1,005 League appearances and almost 1,400 first-class appearances in all. He had also played for England a record 125 times, a figure which would have been much higher had it not been for the emergence of Ray Clemence.

Few would argue that Peter Shilton is one of England's most accomplished goalkeepers of all time. A remarkable schoolboy, he became one of the few to turn outstanding promise into brilliant reality. Commanding, agile and always extremely fit, he had an amazingly safe pair of hands. Shilton displaced Gordon Banks whilst still a teenager at Leicester and became the club's youngest ever first-team player. He was only 16 when he made his debut against Everton, but it was at Nottingham Forest that he won many of his domestic honours – the highlights of which were the League Championship in 1978, and the European Cup in 1979 and 1980, when he stopped just about everything that came his way.

Peter Shilton won his first senior England cap in November 1970. During

1980 and 1981 he conceded just one goal in four qualifying games leading to the 1982 World Cup finals, and then kept four clean sheets in the five games played thereafter.

Shilton kept six clean sheets in the eight qualifying games leading to the 1986 World Cup finals. He did pretty well when the team got to Mexico as well, conceding just one goal in the three Group F games, and keeping a clean sheet as England beat Paraguay 3-0 in the second round match.

But then came the quarter-final against Argentina - and England went out of the competition as Maradona proved that he was quite good with his hands too. Peter Shilton at last left the international stage after helping England reach the 1990 World Cup semi-finals. His last international was a 2-1 defeat by Italy in the third place play-off. It had been some international career.

LEFT Shilton takes a break during the 1990 World Cup, his international swansong

BELOW Entering the Guinness Book of Records at Leyton Orient while registering the 1,000th League game of his career

Throw-ins

IT WAS THE SHEFFIELD FA (UNDER whose rules the Sheffield side, the world's oldest football club having been formed in 1857, play) that first introduced the notion of a throw-in to restart the match after it had gone over the touchline. The FA's rules had dictated a kick-in, similar to a goal kick, but having observed the Sheffield rules subsequently adopted a similar ruling.

To begin with, there were no restrictions on the throw-in; players threw the ball one-handed, similar to a goalkeeper's throw-out and achieved similar distance. In time, the more accepted two-hand, both feet on the ground ruling was adopted.

There are some players to whom the two-handed throw is seen as little or no disadvantage. One of the most comical moments of the 2002-03 season was the sight of Aston Villa goalkeeper Peter Enckelman misjudging a throw-in from one of his defenders and missing the ball as it headed towards his goal. Although Enckelman did not touch the ball (it is not possible to score direct from a throw-in), the referee believed he did, judging by his desperate attempts to retrieve it, and the goal stood.

Chelsea in the 1970s had a long-throw specialist in Ian Hutchinson with his windmill-like action, while Tranmere, who had Dave Challinor two decades later, stationed ball boys around the pitch armed with towels with which he could dry the ball, move the advertising hoardings and launch what was almost the equal of a corner into the opposition penalty area.

Although FIFA tried out a replacement kick in a junior tournament in 1993, these plans were subsequently scrapped. Given the histrionics we see at corners, perhaps FIFA are right to leave the throw-in well alone!

Television

WITH WALL-TO-WALL MATCHES, starting at 12 noon and sometimes not ending until 10pm, it is hard to recall the time when television and football did not go hand in-hand. Indeed, television and football did not develop a proper relationship until somewhat late in the day.

The first FA Cup Final to be broadcast live was the 1938 clash between Preston North End and Huddersfield Town, but there were more people in attendance at the match – 100,000 – than saw the game on television, there being less than 10,000 sets in the country. Even fewer had seen some of the earlier attempts at broadcasting live matches, a 1936 encounter between Arsenal and Everton probably the first.

It was highlights programme Match Of The Day that fuelled real interest in the game, the first programme going out on BBC2 in August 1964 with highlights of Liverpool's home win over Arsenal. Viewing figures of 75,000 were only slightly higher than those who attended the match, but the programme soon became a ratings winner, prompting the rival independent network to launch their own highlights programme.

I t was to take until 1983 before regular live football made its appearance on the programme schedule, with Spurs' home match against Nottingham Forest switched to a Sunday in October with little or no impact on the gate. But at the start of the 1985-86 season the football authorities were unable to conclude a deal with TV and so the screens remained blank.

The arrival of Sky changed the game; it could be said that the Premiership came into being because of television. Not every deal has worked out, as with the League and Carlton/Granada, but TV football is here to stay.

BELOW The action unfolds under the television camera's all-seeing gaze.

BELOW The action unfolds under the television camera's all-seeing gaze.

Transfers

ALMOST AS SOON AS FOOTBALL began to get itself organised, clubs have offered ever-increasing sums in order to secure the services of one player or another. It was in 1908 that the first attempt to control the transfer fee was made, a ceiling of £350 being set by the Football Association as a result of Alf Common becoming the first player to be transferred between clubs for £1,000. This soon proved to be unworkable, with clubs throwing in reserve players and claiming that they were worth the full £350, so the ceiling was abandoned three months later.

Thereafter the transfer limit grew and grew. The first five-figure fee was paid by Arsenal to Bolton Wanderers in 1928 for David Jack and was for £10,890, £10,340 or £10,670 depending on sources. Just short of 30 years later John Charles was the first player to be transferred for more than £50,000, Italian side Juventus paying £65,000 for his signature in June 1957. It was another three years before one English club paid another more than £50,000, Denis Law costing Manchester City this sum.

A little over a year later, Law's value had rocketed, at least as far as Torino were concerned, paying £100,000 to take the striker to Italy in July 1961. Law had 12 months in Italy before he returned home, to Manchester United, for £115,000 to become the first player bought by an English club for in excess of £100,000 (Jimmy Greaves might have been the first some months earlier, but Bill Nicholson deliberately held out for a transfer fee of £99,999 in order to prevent Greaves being labelled the first £100,000 player when moving from AC Milan to Spurs).

The next two milestones were reached within weeks of each other. In June 1977 Kevin Keegan was transferred from Liverpool to Hamburg for £500,000, and in January 1979 David Mills became the first player to switch between English clubs for this sum when West Bromwich Albion paid Middlesbrough £510,000 for his services. Five weeks later, Nottingham Forest paid Birmingham City £975,000 for Trevor Francis, VAT and the player's percentage taking the final bill to £1,150,000.

At present the British record is the £30 million Manchester United paid Leeds United for Rio Ferdinand, but this is still only the sixth highest fee paid in the world, Real Madrid paying Juventus £45.6 million for Zinedine Zidane, only a year after they had paid Barcelona £37.4 million for Luis Figo.

BELOW Britain's most expensive player, Manchester United's Rio Ferdinand

Uruguay

Uruguay in early World Cup action, scoring against Argentina in the 1930 Final

WINSTON CHURCHILL ONCE described Russia as "a riddle wrapped in a mystery inside an enigma." He could just so readily have been describing Uruguay, a country whose abilities as a footballing nation vary between the sublime and the ridiculous.

The first country to win the World Cup, their exploits for the 50 or so years have seen them leading disciples of the cynical football of the 1960s through to a talented side in keeping with their South American heritage.

Uruguay first emerged as a world power towards the end of the 1920s when they won the gold for football at the 1928 Olympics at Amsterdam. The success of the tournament prompted FIFA to finally institute a World Cup competition, to be held in Uruguay in 1930. Organised on a straight knock-out basis, Uruguay made it to the Final to play their closest neighbours and rivals Argentina and won 4-2. However, as most of the major European footballing nations had not bothered to make the journey to South America, Uruguay refused to journey to Italy to defend the Jules Rimet trophy in 1934! They stayed away again in 1938, returning to the fold in 1950 in Brazil.

Required to play only one qualifying match, in which they beat Bolivia 8-0, Uruguay took their place in the final pool along with Brazil, Sweden and Spain. A draw against Spain and one-goal victory over Sweden preceded a game (effectively the Final) against a Brazilian side that had won both of their matches against Spain and Sweden. It meant Brazil needed only a draw to be crowned world champions, whilst Uruguay would have to quieten 200,000 Brazilians squeezed into the Maracana Stadium. After a goalless first half, Brazil took the lead and seemingly the title, but goals from Schiaffino and Ghiggia took the trophy to Montevideo for the second and so far last time.

Semi-finalists in Switzerland in 1954 (where they were beaten by the Mighty Magyars), Uruguay next made an impact, albeit for all the wrong reasons, in 1966. Qualifiers, along with England from Group 1, Uruguay were pitted against the West Germans in the quarter-final. Their battle was virtually a mirror image of the European/South American clash going on between England and Argentina at Wembley; Uruguay hit the bar, had a good penalty claim turned down and lost their heads, two men and four goals in a heated second half.

Better behaved and better rewarded in 1970, they made it as far as the semi-final before bowing out to the Brazilians. That proved to be their last meaningful contribution to the World Cup finals, for although they have qualified three further times (once via the play-offs against Australia) they have not progressed beyond the first round.

United

MANCHESTER UNITED WAS founded in 1878, when the club was known as Newton Heath. During the early years of the twentieth century, United largely played second fiddle to Manchester City. This was also the case in the 1930s, when City spent every season except the last in the top division, while United were mainly a Second Division side. In 1934, United finished 21st in the old Second Division, and only narrowly avoided relegation to Division Three (North) while, at the end of that same season, City achieved 5th place in Division One.

Everything was to change after World War Two. United gradually came to reign supreme in Manchester and, in 1952, they won their first League Championship for 41 years. They won it twice more during the 1950s, and twice during the 1960s. After that however, the top spot was to elude them until 1993, although they did come close to it on a few occasions. United were champions of the newly formed Premier League in 1993, and they retained the Championship the following year.

ABOVE David Sadler beats George Best to hoist the European Cup aloft, Wembley, 1968

ABOVE RIGHT Fergie's Fledglings now rival the Busby Babes as the greatest United team ever

Between 1993 and 2003 they won the Premiership title on no fewer that eight occasions, also winning the FA Cup three times.

Manchester United had won the European Cup in 1968, when they beat Benfica 4-1 (after extra time) at Wembley, and they were to win the European championship again in 1999. They beat Bayern Munich 2-1 at the Nou Camp, and in that year completed the unique Treble of Premiership, FA Cup, and European titles.

Manchester United's record is of course an excellent one. United are the best known club side on earth, and they have supporters' clubs all over the globe. They won the Premiership title in season 2002-03, but the 2003-04 campaign was a difficult one – though they did win the FA Cup Final in which they beat Millwall. Rumours and speculation regarding a takeover bid probably affected the players, and the team was clearly missing the skills of David Beckham. Watch this space.

UEFA

IT WAS 50 YEARS AFTER THE formation of FIFA that Europe, always the motivating force, felt compelled to organise the Union of European Football Associations (UEFA) in 1954. To begin with, UEFA had no intention of organising competitions; this was to be almost imposed upon them.

The success of the European Champions' Clubs Cup (the name 'European Cup' was to have been used for a national competition) prompted the launch of a similar competition for national cup winners, the European Cup Winners' Cup. Although there was a third competition, the Inter-Cities Fairs Cup, this was never organised by UEFA and is not recognised by them as an official competition! That all changed in 1971 with the creation of the UEFA Cup.

Today UEFA, which has 52 members, organises 15 competitions, nine for national representative sides and six for clubs, which range from the European Championships and European Champions League through to a continental championship for five-a-side football, taking in a women's competition along the way.

When formed, UEFA had 25 national association members; subsequent political changes in Eastern Europe have more than doubled that number. More importantly, interest in its competitions, particularly the European Championships, has increased ten-fold.

BELOW UEFA supremo Lennart Johansson talks shop. The organisation he heads celebrated its half-century in 2004

Van Nistelrooy

MANCHESTER UNITED'S STAR striker Ruud van Nistelrooy was born in Oss, Holland, on 1st July 1976. He was not always a goalscorer, and it took a little while for his game to develop. Having started as a sweeper, he joined Dutch Second Division side FC Den Bosch, where he occupied a midfield role, lurking behind the forward line. Four years later he transferred to First Division SC Heerenveen, where he became a striker but not yet an outstanding performer.

The coach at Heerenveen sent him to watch Dennis Bergkamp in action. Van Nistelrooy was determined to succeed, and he learned a great deal. In fact, he learned so much that, on his 22nd birthday, PSV Eindhoven paid a domestic record fee of £4.2 million to secure his signature. The van Nistelrooy bandwagon was now well and truly rolling,

and in November 1998 he made his first international appearance. During that season, he was top scorer in the Dutch League, netting on 31 occasions.

The Premiership beckoned, but first the Dutch striker had to overcome serious injury. A ruptured cruciate ligament caused him to miss out on Euro 2000 and for a while there were fears that he might never be the same player again. Alex Ferguson had his beady eye on him, however, and when van Nistelrooy eventually regained full fitness he was signed by United in April 2001 for a massive £19 million fee.

Ruud van Nistelrooy had a remarkable first season at Old Trafford. He scored 36 goals in all competitions, an incredible tally considering he had only recently recovered from his major knee problem. In season 2002-03, he went eight better, netting on 44 occasions as the Reds won the Premiership title.

He was a little less prolific in 2003-04, as United stuttered and he lacked those precision Beckham passes. Transfer speculation linked him with both Spanish giants, Real and Barcelona, but wherever he plays his football Van the Man will expect to score a lot more goals in the future.

Villa

ASTON VILLA, BIRMINGHAM'S senior club by the matter of a single year, have been one of English football's biggest for as long as the game has been played, though in recent decades they have under-achieved in relation to their stalwart support. Their status has also been enhanced by Villa Park, a ground regularly used to stage FA Cup semi-finals and, in 1996, European Championship games.

Villa became only the second club ever to win the League and Cup Double in 1897, thanks to the goals of John Campbell and George Wheldon. More recently, they won the European Cup in 1982 under assistant manager Tony Barton (Ron Saunders having resigned earlier in the season) to signal a brief return to the heady heights of those early glory days.

Their other highlight of recent years came in 1990 when Graham Taylor took them to second in the top flight, having obtained promotion the previous season, but he was poached to become England manager. The series of men who replaced him – Ron Atkinson, John

BELOW The goals of
Columbian hitman Juan
Pablo Angel helped his
club, Aston Villa, to a
highly respectable
Premiership placing in
season 2003-04

Gregory and Josef Venglos among them – proved inadequate for the task, and though Taylor himself returned for a second, less successful spell it wasn't until the appointment of David O'Leary in 2003 that the club threatened to return to the top echelons of the domestic game.

They have young England hopefuls like Jlloyd Samuel and the now established Darius Vassell together with the finally firing Colombian Juan Pablo Angel and Danish keeper Thomas Sorensen. All will need to be retained, while long-time owner Doug Ellis will need to loosen the purse strings if another European Cup adventure is to be enjoyed in the foreseeable future. There is also the crucial matter of confirming what Villa fans see as their traditional position as Birmingham's top team, with Steve Bruce's Blues also in the ascendancy at the time of writing.

Van Basten

HAVING HELPED FIRST CLUB AJAX win the Dutch league in his first full season, 1982-83, Marco Van Basten (born 31st October 1964 in Utrecht, Holland) made his big breakthrough in the 1983-84 campaign when he scored 28 goals in 26 games. His combination of power and pace, allied with a shrewd footballing brain, made him nearly impossible to defend against.

Having made 143 League appearances and scored 128 times for Ajax, a stunning goals to games ratio, he signed for AC Milan in 1987-88 but was immediately afflicted by an ankle injury.

The 1988 European Championships gave him the chance to make an improbably swift comeback, setting up Holland's first goal against Russia in the Final and scoring the second with a memorable volley from an impossible angle. He finished the competition's top scorer with five and finished a supposedly dead season World Footballer of the Year.

But 1992's European Championship Final was a very different matter. Holland lost against Denmark, Marco missing a penalty. He enjoyed better fortune in club football, however, and Milan took the European Cup in successive years 1989 and 1990, following through with the World Club Cup.

In-between injuries, the player scored an incredible 90 goals in 147 Serie A games (including 25 in 1991-92, a personal record) and had a better than 90 per cent conversion record at penalties, a statistic that made his European Championship failure against Peter Schmeichel the more inexplicable.

Van Basten, who retired through injury in 1995, was selected as the best player in Europe in 1988, 1989 and 1992. He returned to his first club and currently coaches Ajax Youth, passing on his skills to a new generation.

BELOW Marco Van Basten, Holland's best ever out-and-out striker, celebrates his ultimate season in 1988

World Cup

RIGHT The current World Cup was adopted after then three-time winners Brazil were awarded the Jules Rimet trophy in perpetuity

IT WAS JULES RIMET, THE president of the World Football Federation, who started it all. Aided by a small committee, he organised the first tournament which took place in Uruguay in 1930. Only a handful of European countries took part and the home nation won the tournament, beating Argentina 4-2 in the Final. It was a relatively small beginning but Monsieur Rimet had a vision. He believed that "Soccer could reinforce the ideals of a permanent and real peace" and, although he may have got this a little wrong, his tournament was to take off in a very big way.

Another home nation, this time Italy, won the Cup in 1934, and the Italians have now lifted the trophy on three occasions. Top of the league however, come five-times winners Brazil, West Germany, like Italy, having won it three times. The World Cup has been won twice by Argentina and Uruguay, and once by France.

England's only success came, as everyone knows, in 1966. Alf Ramsay had fashioned his team of 'wingless wonders' and truly believed that the ultimate triumph was possible. At times it seemed unlikely, but a quarter-final

victory over Argentina and a semi-final win against Portugal meant that England reached the Final. West Germany were to prove hard to beat, but Alf believed.

The Germans took the lead in the first half, but Geoff Hurst had levelled the score by the interval. Martin Peters made it 2-1 in the second period and, as the minutes ticked by, it seemed that it was all over – but then, following a free kick, West Germany scored again, just seconds from the end of normal time. The rest is, of course, history. Alf rallied his troops, and in extra time (and with the approval of a friendly Russian linesman) Geoff Hurst scored England's third. Hurst then completed his hat trick and, at 4-2, it really was all over. We haven't done quite so well since.

Wembley

THE EMPIRE STADIUM, WEMBLEY, was completed early in 1923. With its impressive twin towers it was, at the time, the most impressive stadium in the world and could hold more than 100,000 spectators. As it could cope with so many people, it was not thought necessary to make its first big game, the 1923 FA Cup Final, an all-ticket affair.

RIGHT Crowd control at Wembley's first FA Cup Final, 1923.

OPPOSITE The new and controversial Wembley takes shape, its new tubular arch clearly visible

BELOW An aerial view of Wembley during the 1923 Cup Final, showing the twin towers on the right

The result was that about a quarter of a million fans turned up to see Bolton Wanderers play West Ham, and they almost took part in a national disaster. In the event, this was avoided by allowing large numbers of people onto the pitch and controlling them with an army of mounted policemen. The official attendance figure was 126,047, but it's certain that the real figure was much higher.

Wembley hosted the Olympic Games in 1948, and the World Cup Final of 1966. However, after 1923, its main claim to fame was as the venue for the FA Cup Final. Every club wanted to 'get to Wembley' and the old place staged the final until the end of the century. By then it was in sore need of reconstruction, and eventually the decision was taken to pull it down and start all over again.

The rebuilding of Wembley has been a long and tortuous process. Much has gone wrong, and the whole area became a very large building site. The

twin towers have disappeared for ever, but in their place there will one day be a new and technically advanced 90,000 all-seater stadium. A steel arch will surmount a sliding roof and there will be two enormous TV screens for the showing of action replays. Corporate hospitality will of course loom large, but hopefully genuine football supporters will still be able to afford to watch their team win or lose the Cup. The final cost of the new Wembley Stadium will be astronomical, but it is currently due for completion by the year 2006.

Wales

TRADITIONALLY, WELSH SOCCER has always been in the shadow of rugby football and it used to be seen by many Welshmen as a second-class sport. The decline in the fortunes of Welsh rugby did, however, coincide to an extent with increasing interest in the round-ball game and, over the past 50 years or so, the Principality has produced some excellent players.

The most notable of these was inside forward Ivor Allchurch. Born in Swansea, he made 330 League appearances for his home-town club, before moving on to Newcastle and then Cardiff. He finished his career back in Swansea in 1968, but in-between times he played 68 times for Wales. Ivor was very quick, had excellent ball control, and was a prolific goal scorer – netting 251 times in a total of 682 League appearances. His brother Len, an outside-right, was also a very good footballer and he won 11 Welsh caps. Centre-half Mel Nurse was another Swansea boy who made the big time with Swansea, Middlesborough and Swindon, and played for Wales on 12 occasions.

More recently, Wales has produced the likes of Ian Rush and Ryan Giggs. Superb striker Rush made 658 appearances for Liverpool, scoring 346 goals in his two spells with the club. He moved briefly to Juventus, but whilst at Anfield he played 73 times for his country. Manchester United's Ryan Giggs is still

BELOW Current Wales manager Mark Hughes can boast 72 caps as a player between 1984 and 1999

RIGHT Cardiff striker
Robert Earnshaw,
pictured playing against
Scotland, has a bright
international future
with Wales

going strong and, when he is allowed to play for Wales, he does a tremendous job in midfield.

On the international front, Wales have recorded comparatively little success, although recent performances have often been a lot better than many outside the Principality expected. The most notable achievement came in the 1958 World Cup when, against all the odds, Wales progressed to the last eight. Brazil were their quarter-final opponents and, had it not been for a rather accomplished 17-year-old player called Pelé, who scored the game's only goal, they might well have progressed further. With Mark Hughes at the helm, they only just failed to qualify for Euro 2004, after playing off with Russia, and in the likes of Robert Earnshaw, who notched a hat-trick against Scotland in early 2004, they have the foundations for a bright future playing at the impressive Millennium Stadium.

X-Tra time

THERE IS NO RECORD AS TO when extra time was first introduced as a way of trying to separate two sides who had drawn a cup tie. We do know that in 1898 Sheffield United refused to play an extra half-hour in a replay of the Sheriff of London's Shield (a forerunner to the FA Charity Shield), but this was in protest at some of the referee's decisions.

A law establishing extra time was introduced by the FA Council in 1912, although initially this was purely for the Final itself. It was not until 1920 that extra time was first used in the FA Cup Final, when Aston Villa and Huddersfield Town had battled for 90 minutes without either side scoring a goal. The players were obviously unsure of the arrangements as they all shook hands and walked off! It was the referee who pointed out that they had another half-hour to go, upon which they returned to the field, Kirton of Villa finally managing to break the deadlock.

ABOVE Geoff Hurst hits England's third goal in extra time to break the 1966 World Cup Final deadlock

Since extra time was introduced into all competitions, most of the real action has taken place in the added half-hour. As lively as the first 90 minutes was in the 1966 World Cup Final between England and West Germany, it was the two goals, one contentious, the other clear-cut, that has remained in the memory.

Similarly, the semi-final clash between West Germany and Italy four years later, which finally resulted in a 4-3 win for the Italians, belied the (lack of) action that had preceded it.

Recent attempts to modify the system

RIGHT All pools coupons had to be checked individually by hand in the pre-computerised era

have seen the introduction of silver and golden goals. With silver goals, if a team scores in the first half of extra time and is still leading at half-time, then they are declared the winners. With golden goals, the side that scores first irrespective of when it occurs are declared the winners. Why not just carry on for the full half-hour – experience has shown that there is still time for a side to score, even in the last minute of extra time and rescue a match that was seemingly lost 20 minutes previously. If golden goals are to be introduced, why not have the system operate after half an hour's extra time has been played?

X marks the spot

IT WAS A SCENE REPEATED IN households around the country; every Saturday afternoon, at 4.45, fathers and grandfathers would huddle around the radio or, if they were well off, the television set, and listen with great intent to the football results.

In households in Torquay, what mattered most was not the performance of their own hometown team, but had

Hartlepool managed to gain a creditable draw at Chesterfield? Meanwhile, in Hartlepool, they were more concerned with whether Fulham had come from behind to rescue a point at Portsmouth.

Before the national lottery and with the possible exception of the premium bond, the only way to (legally) acquire an instant fortune was predicting scores via the football pools.

They had been launched in 1923 by John Moores and two friends, all telegraphists, who invested £50 each and printed up four thousand football coupons, which they distributed outside Manchester United's ground one Saturday afternoon. Only 35 of these were returned, with stake money of £5, and £2 of this was paid out in winnings in that first week.

By the end of the season, the venture had incurred losses of £600, a phenomenal amount for the time, and two of the group decided to cut their losses and move onto something else. John

Moores, who called his company Littlewoods Pools, carried on alone and by the time he was 35 had made himself a millionaire.

Along the way he attracted competition, Vernons started in 1925 and Zetters in 1933, but it has always been Littlewoods that promised the biggest jackpots and, at times, the larger-than-life characters that won them.

Unlike betting on horses or other sports, the football pools have always appeared complex. You are not trying to guess which team will beat another, but which matches will end in draws! The popularity of the football pools was such that at its height, more than a billion coupons would be entered each season, and each of these would have to be checked by hand.

There were one or two spectacular winners too, most notably the Nicholson family in 1961. Miner Keith Nicholson and his liquorice factory-worker wife Viv scooped a jackpot of £152,000 (equal to £3 million in today's money) and, when asked what they intended doing with the money, replied "Spend, spend, spend."

Keith was killed in a car crash on his way to meet his racehorse trainer four

LEFT The rich but ultimately tragic figure of 1961 pools winner Viv Nicholson years later and Viv had soon lost not only her husband but most of his money.

The launch of the national lottery, which offered greater jackpots for even less work, slashed interest in the football pools overnight (in 2001 Littlewoods' income from the pools was £44 million; by comparison, Camelot's from the lottery was £4.98 billion).

Despite this, there are still two million people a week who play the football pools, still dreaming of winning the jackpot, still hoping Hartlepool get a draw at Chesterfield.

X-certificate

The various football authorities have done their best to clean the game up on the pitch, making almost every offence punishable by a yellow card and a red for subsequent misdemeanours. The tackle from behind has been outlawed, as has the two-footed challenge, raising the elbows, challenging the goalkeeper – in fact, almost everything that was once used to halt the game or slow the pace right down.

Perhaps the earliest match affected by a free for all was the 1905 League match between Manchester City and Aston Villa. City were pushing for the title and needed to win, but Villa triumphed on the day 3-2 in a match that was frequently interrupted by Sandy Turnbull and Andy Leake trading punches. An FA commission was set up to look into the affair and three months later announced that Billy Meredith, who had taken no part in the match, was to be banned for one season for attempting to bribe a Villa player!

In 1934 England met Italy in a 'friendly' at Highbury, a match made all the more intriguing by virtue of the Italians having recently won the World Cup. England included in their side seven Arsenal players, the most representatives from one club and, familiar with the playing style of their side, soon raced into a three-goal lead.

The Italians then lost their heads and the second half was little more than a shambles, with scuffles breaking out here and there as players sought instant retribution. Although England won the match 3-1, the whole affair became notorious as the Battle of Highbury.

This was a picnic compared with the

LEFT Argentine captain
Antonio Rattin receives
his marching orders
against England, 1966

World Cup match between Brazil and Hungary in Berne in 1954. English referee Arthur Ellis put the first name in his notebook soon after kick-off and was the busiest man on the field, for at the end of 90 minutes had had to send three players off and give repeated instructions to cool down to just about everyone else.

Aside from five goals (the match was won by the Hungarians 3-2), most of the action wouldn't have been out of place in a boxing ring, and all the players were involved in another free-for-all in the corridor and dressing rooms after the match had officially ended!

Whilst only three players received their marching orders during this tempestuous affair, they had a long way to go to match the activities of the Chilean and Uruguayan sides involved in a so-called friendly match in 1975 – the game had to be abandoned after 19 players had been sent off – nine from Uruguay and ten from Chile!

Whilst most of the punch-ups that occur on a football field involve members of opposing sides, Mike Flanagan and Derek Hales, sent off during a Cup tie between Charlton and Maidstone United, were both playing for Charlton. Flanagan was fined £250 and Hales sacked (though later reinstated). It makes the censures issued after brawls between Arsenal and Manchester United in recent years seem tame by comparison...

RIGHT The
incomparable Lev
Yashin in action

Yashin

SOVIET GOALKEEPER LEV YASHIN, born in October 1929, cut an imposing figure in his all-black kit. Nicknamed the Octopus in celebration of his all-encompassing handling, he was a fixture on the international scene behind the red-shirted Russian defence from the mid 1950s to 1967. Yet it could have been so different: disillusioned by his inability to make the Moscow Dynamo first eleven, he considered switching sports to ice hockey (where he also kept goal) in 1953. Happily, he was not lost to football and Dynamo would be his only team after he finally displaced Tiger Khomich for both club and, eventually, country.

Yashin created a record in achieving 78 international caps, winning the 1956 Olympics and the 1960 European Championship with his country as well as finishing third in the 1966 World Cup

– the third finals in which he'd participated. Little wonder his country gave him its top honour, the Order of Lenin, in 1968, the year after he bowed out of international football. (Such was his reputation, however, that he travelled to Mexico in 1970 as third-choice keeper and goodwill aide.)

An outstanding athlete, he possessed agility and anticipation paralleled by few other goalkeepers, and his shot-stopping was outstanding: it is claimed he kept 270 clean sheets and saved over 150 penalties during his career. He retired in 1971 at 41 years of age, a team of European stars playing an exhibition match in his honour at the Lenin Stadium. One of his best-recalled performances had been in another such game, the 1963 FA Centenary match in which he appeared as keeper for the Rest of the World against England at Wembley, making a number of the breathtaking saves.

As well as helping Dynamo to many League and Cup triumphs, Yashin won the 1963 European Player of the Year award – the only goalkeeper ever to have won that prize. He had a leg amputated in 1986, the legacy of a knee injury, and died in 1990. A statue was erected in his memory at Dinamo Central Stadium in Moscow.

Youth Football

Many lower-league football clubs have ensured their survival by capturing young talent, nurturing such players

ABOVE Coach Hugh McAuley leads Liverpool's Academy players in a warm-up jogging session

and then selling them on to bigger, richer clubs. Unfortunately, the game plan changed somewhat with the advent of the Bosman ruling which allowed players over the age of 23 to move on free at the end of their contract unlike the 'retain and transfer' system that had previously held sway. Even if young players were still subject to compensation payment, it all restricted the ability of clubs to fund the youth systems on which they had relied.

Scotland has been particularly hard-hit by cheap foreign imports in the domestic game whose arrival reduced the chances of young home-grown players breaking through. The Scottish FA acted by imposing an under-21 rule on Scottish Premier reserve games, with only a bare minimum of over-age players being allowed per team.

The training that takes place in the Academy of a Premier League club on either side of the border follows a technical programme carefully tailored to suit the still developing bodies of the young players. The method is based on guided repetition, where skills are repeated continuously until techniques are mastered. Drills allow players maximum contact with the ball and emphasis is placed on individual progress rather than match results, long-term development the aim.

Football Academies help the players through their various stages of physical development, particularly with respect to posture, balance and body positioning, aiming to build strong bodies that will be resistant to injury and recover quickly following games.

But becoming a professional player is an extremely difficult task and there are no guarantees of success. Consequently, Academy players are encouraged to develop a wide range of skills through the educational and core skills programme so that if a player leaves without a professional contract they can still reflect on their experience as being a productive one. They also receive support in finding new clubs and/or careers.

You'll Never Walk Alone

WHEN AMERICAN OSCAR Hammerstein II first read Ferenc Molnar's play *Liliom* and then penned some lyrics for his friend Richard Rogers' musical *Carousel*, which was based on that play, he could never have believed that his little song would one day become the anthem of Liverpool Football Club. But that's football for you.

When local pop favourite Gerry Marsden covered the song, which topped the chart in 1963, with his Pacemakers, he unwittingly started a trend which continues to this day. When you attended a football match prior to the 1960s, you heard little or no singing. Most people stood on the terraces and came up with no more than an occasional insult (often referring to the doubtful parentage of the referee) an occasional witticism and, on a good day, a bit of half-hearted chanting. Basically, you cheered, clapped or moaned, according to the state of the game, and then you either went for a pint or, more likely, home to the wife for a nice cup of tea. Those were indeed the days.

Singing and chanting is now a part of football, and it serves a dual purpose. Popular culture dictates that everyone should be fond of popular music, although there is not much that is musical about some of the singing heard at Premiership grounds, and there can be little doubt that singing and chanting encourages the players in their endeavours. It's all about atmosphere, and it also helps the bonding process amongst supporters, assuming they need it.

There does however seem to be a paucity of good tunes as, time after time, fans adapt the same old song to their own local circumstances: and so we have 'Cheer Up Kevin Keegan', or Graham Souness, or almost any other manager who appears to be in a spot of bother. It's not very inventive, so all credit to the Liverpool fans who first adopted 'You'll Never Walk Alone'. It happens to be a very good song – so good that Celtic have borrowed it in recent years.

BELOW The Anfield Kop, whose rendition of 'You'll Never Walk Alone' has become internationally famous

Zola

THE DIMINUTIVE GIANFRANCO Zola joined Chelsea Football Club in November 1997. Born in Oliena, Sardinia on 5th July 1966, he had been the successor to the equally diminutive, and far less resilient, Diego Maradona at Napoli. Whilst in southern Italy Zola had won an Italian Championship medal, and he later picked up a UEFA Cup winner's medal with Parma. He had 26 Italian caps to his credit by the time he arrived at Stamford Bridge as a 31 year-old, but Gianfranco still had a great deal to offer.

Zola was a hard worker, read the game beautifully and showed tremendous vision as, in his first season at Chelsea, he helped his team to win both the European Cup Winners' Cup and the League Cup. However, his second and third seasons at the Bridge were rather less impressive, although he helped Chelsea win the FA Cup in 1999-2000. By the summer of 2002, he felt it was time to call it a day and return to Sardinia.

Chelsea fans did not want to lose him and neither did the club itself, and in the end he was persuaded to stay on for another year. It proved to be a good decision for both club and player.

At the age of 37, and having played in 266 games for Chelsea, scoring a total of 64 goals, he finally returned to his beloved island home in 2003.

Zoff

GOALKEEPER DINO ZOFF (BORN in February 1942) found fame relatively late in life. After playing lower-division football for Udinese and Mantova a move to Napoli put him in the spotlight, but it was joining Juventus for a record fee for a keeper in 1972 that lit the touch paper. He would go on to notch five League and two Cup wins, as well as the UEFA Cup (1977) with Juve.

In the colours of his country Zoff would win the European Championship in 1968, having made his debut in the quarter-final against Bulgaria. He retained his place in the semi-final and Final against Yugoslavia but didn't make the team for the 1970 World Cup finals.

Undeterred, Zoff captained Italy to World Cup victory in Spain in 1982 at the age of 40, having earlier created a world record for not conceding an international goal from September 1972 to June 1974, a total of 1,142 minutes.

He cut his managerial teeth in Rome with Lazio (where he signed Paul Gascoigne) before taking on the national team in December 1999. His attempt to match Franz Beckenbauer's record as the only man to captain and manage a European Championship-winning side was just 20 seconds from fruition before 2000 home nation France stole his thunder. Zoff briefly rejoined Lazio for a second managerial-spell, replacing Sven Goran Eriksson.

BELOW Captain and keeper Dino Zoff, in grey, joins the World Cup celebrations, 1982

Zidane

ANYONE WHO COULD KEEP Eric Cantona in his prime out of the French national squad had to be an exceptional footballer. Ironically, Zinedine Zidane was born, like Cantona, in the southern French port of Marseilles and, though pursuing a less controversial path, proved himself one of the world's great footballers.

He started professional life with Cannes before deciding to go west to Bordeaux in 1992. At the beginning of his third season with Les Girondins he was given his international debut and promptly scored two brilliant goals in a 2-2 draw with the Czech Republic on his home turf in Bordeaux's Parc Lescure. Almost at once the French press began to compare him with the great Michel Platini.

By the summer of 1996 Zidane was national coach Aimé Jacquet's first-choice playmaker. He had enjoyed his best season yet for Bordeaux, helping the club to reach the Final of the UEFA Cup with some breathtaking passing and spectacular goals.

At Euro '96 in England, he looked tired after a long, arduous season and failed to deliver the goods. But Italian

RIGHT The incomparable Zinedine Zidane in World Cup action for France against Japan, 2002

giants Juventus had already agreed to pay Bordeaux £3.2 million for his services, and 'Zizou' quickly recaptured his best form in the famous black and white stripes, helping Juve challenge strongly on both domestic and European fronts. His efforts in steering them to two Champions League Finals were rewarded with the 1998 Footballer of the Year award – recognition too of his leadership in that year's World Cup.

France were expected to retain the world crown in 2002, especially having won Euro 2000 on home turf, but their inspiration struggled against injury in the Far East as his side were sent packing after the first round.

A move to Real Madrid in 2001 for a world record £45.6 million fee rejuvenated his career, and Champions League victory in 2002 was just reward for his efforts.

Now playing alongside similar world-class talents in Beckham, Roberto Carlos and Luis Figo, there may well be more glory to come.

BELOW The world's most expensive footballer at £45.6 million pictured in action for Real Madrid

The pictures in this book were provided courtesy of the following:

GETTY IMAGES
101 Bayham Street, London NW1 0AG

POPPERFOTO.COM
The Old Mill, Overstone Farm, Northampton NN6 0AB

Book design and artwork by Simon Joslin
Based on a design by Darren Roberts

Published by Green Umbrella

Series Editors Jules Gammond and Tim Exell

Written by Michael Heatley with Graham Betts and Chris Mason